ESOP

REGULATORY RULINGS

1990–2024

Corey Rosen

The National Center for Employee Ownership (NCEO)

Visit **www.nceo.org** for more information about employee ownership, ownership culture, and leadership

This publication is designed to provide accurate and authoritative information in regard to the subject matter covered. It is sold with the understanding that the author and the publisher are not engaged in rendering legal, accounting, or other professional advice, and that other people in the field may disagree about some of the statements made about the cases summarized here. If legal advice or other expert assistance is required, the services of a competent professional should be sought.

We have made reasonable attempts to include all relevant rulings within the given time period, but we cannot guarantee that we have included every one. Practitioners should use this as a starting point and conduct their own research.

The National Center for Employee Ownership (NCEO)
510-208-1300
Email: customerservice@nceo.org
Web: www.nceo.org

ISBN 978-1-954990-39-5

Contents

Introduction

The purpose of this publication is to provide practitioners and other interested people with a summary of rulings on ESOPs and related plans. Regulations issued by the Internal Revenue Service (IRS) and U.S. Department of Labor (DOL) can be very detailed, ranging from a few pages to dozens of pages or more. We have not tried to summarize them in any detail here but rather to highlight key issues and describe what the regulations require. Of course, you can also consult the rulings directly.

In addition to regulations, we have included guidance from the IRS or DOL through IRS private letter rulings (PLRs), DOL advisory opinions, DOL field assistance bulletins, IRS Technical Assistance Memoranda, and similar pronouncements.

IRS private letter rulings and technical assistance memoranda as well as Department of Labor (DOL) advisory opinions do not have regulatory force and deal with the specific facts and circumstances presented. They usually do indicate how the agencies would respond to similar situations, however. DOL field assistance bulletins provide guidance to DOL officials in reviewing plans, but also do not have regulatory force. We have also included "ESOP Cadre Guidance." These were issued starting in 2009. The Cadre is a group of IRS agents providing guidance for the issuance of determination letters. The guidance does not have any legal force but is a good indication of how the IRS would respond to various provisions in ESOP plan documents.

Private letter rulings are listed by their number only, which is how they are typically referenced in other texts. The ruling number always starts with the year (1999, for instance). You can search for the text of these rulings on the IRS site or (often more directly) through a web search. Note, however, that the IRS numbered the PLRs without the first two digits of the year until 1999.

We have categorized the rulings where we believe they best fit. Where a ruling clearly applies in more than one category, we have included it in each applicable category.

Where there are final regulations, we have included the final rulings, not all the interim and temporary rulings that were either changed or finalized by the final regulations.

We have only included rulings specific to ESOPs. There are many other rulings that apply to qualified plans in general. We also do not include such annual updates as cost-of-living adjustments. Every effort has been made to be comprehensive, but it is possible that we have overlooked some rulings. We would appreciate any corrections or additions.

To identify the rulings, we relied primarily on the annual ESOP legal update in the *Journal of Employee Ownership Law and Finance* (which ceased publication in 2011, when it was replaced by NCEO's issue brief series). Material for the first three years of this review came from a compilation by the author. All of the summaries here, however, were written by the author. In addition, we relied on summaries in our newsletter, which in turn relied primarily on information from the *BNA Pension Reporter*. We have, however, found some additional PLRs (but not other rulings) that did not appear, albeit they were very rarely on significant issues. We used the One-Stop ESOP Blog by Aaron Juckett of ESOP Partners, as well as Google searches, to help find these additional PLRs.

It is notable that there were far more ESOP PLRs in the 1990s and early 2000s than since then. In fact, the last IRS private letter ruling or technical advice memorandum on ESOPs or stock bonus plans was in 2017. In part, this is because ESOP legislation and regulation has increasingly clarified what the law requires. There were also a series of similar PLRs on substantial compliance with Section 1042 of the Internal Revenue Code (the "Code") and ESOP dividend deductibility, a number of abusive S ESOP issues, and many PLRs concerning corporate reorganizations in public companies with ESOPs (ESOPs are much less common in public companies today).

The rulings have been categorized according to the main issues they concern. Within each category, the rulings are listed in reverse chronological order. The key issue area for each ruling within a category in italics appears in italics. While we have tried to impose a logical order on the rulings, if you do not find a ruling under the category you first check, you can scan other possible categories quickly to see if the issue shows up elsewhere.

About the 2024 Edition

The original version of this publication appeared in 2011. The 2024 edition adds two items: (1) new guidance issued by the IRS, DOL, and Pension Benefit Guarantee Corporation affecting who must have an annual plan audit effective for plan years starting in 2023 onward, and (2) Rev. Rul. 2003-27 from 2003, requiring the basis of S corporation ESOP shares to be adjusted for net unrealized appreciation calculations.

Accounting

Federal Reserve exempts certain ESOPs from equity requirements. In 12 CFR Part 217, Regulation Q (Dec. 4, 2015), the Board of Governors of the Federal Reserve System issued a final ruling on bank holding companies not organized as stock corporations. As part of that ruling, the Federal Reserve exempted ESOPs in companies that are bank or savings and loan holding companies "until the Board adopts regulations that directly relate to the application of capital regulations to employee stock ownership plans."

Banks and Thrift Institutions

Conversions. Office of Thrift Supervision, Conversions from Mutual to Stock Form, 59 Fed. Reg. 22725: Amended regulations governing mutual-to-stock conversions of insured savings associations, including placing ESOP rights after those of secured depositors.

Capital requirements. The Federal Reserve delayed final action on its revised capital framework under Regulation Q (Regulation Q, 12 CFR part 217). As part of this revision, the Federal Reserve said that it is revising its guidelines on how ESOPs in bank holding companies are treated. Currently, the assets and liabilities of ESOP holding companies are consolidated onto the balance sheet of plan sponsors, some of which are holding companies subject to Regulation Q. Until that review is completed, the Federal Reserve will hold off any decisions about the application of the new tier 1 rules for ESOPs.

Federal Reserve and FirstFed Bancorp agree to termination of enforcement action concerning ESOP. In *Written agreement by and among FirstFed Bancorp, Inc. Employee Stock Ownership Plan, Bessemer, AL, FirstFed Bancorp, Inc., Bessemer, AL, and Federal Reserve Bank of Atlanta, GA,* Docket Nos. 11-070-WA/RB-HC1 11-070-WA/RB-HC2 (Sept. 6, 2016), the Federal Reserve and FirstFed Bancorp Inc. of Bessemer, Alabama, agreed to a procedure in which certain actions will be taken concerning the financial management of the bank to assure that it remains financially sound. The bank will require prior approval from the Federal Reserve of new debt, dividends, acquisition of new capital, and other matters. The bank is a NASDAQ company, and the ESOP is a partial owner.

Contributions

See also leveraged ESOPs section for rulings on Section 415 issues when an ESOP is terminated and shares are redeemed.

Contributions can be combined. PLR 200436015: Ruled that contributions to pay an ESOP loan and separate contributions not used to pay the loan would be defined separately so that the company could make up to a 25% of pay contribution to the non-leveraged portion of the plan and a 25% contribution to pay the principal on the ESOP loan and both would be deductible. The ruling specifically only applies to C corporations. The ruling made it clear that this would only apply if Section 415 limits were not violated.

Deduction denied. IRS Audit (2007, unpublished): The IRS disallowed a deduction of over $1 billion by Marriott for forgiven principal and interest on a leveraged ESOP. Marriott reached a $220 million settlement.

Restorative payments. PLR 200007038: Ruled that a restorative payment pursuant to a lawsuit would not be considered an employer contribution.

Restorative payments. PLR 199913047: Ruled that payments to an ESOP pursuant to the settlement of litigation with the federal government were not contributions that could violate the annual addition limits.

Release of shares. PLR 9847010: Ruled that the receipt of the return of a capital distribution pursuant to an IPO and the subsequent purchase of additional company stock by the ESOP would not result in the release of additional shares from the ESOP loan suspense account or be treated as an "annual addition" under Code Section 415(c).

Contributions can be combined. PLR 9548036: Ruled that a company can contribute up to 25% of eligible leveraged ESOP to pay loan principal plus up to an additional 15% of eligible payroll to a profit-sharing plan, provided that annual addition limits under Section 415 of the Code were not exceeded (this was confirmed in a more recent ruling (PLR 200436015), which updated the number to 25% for each plan to reflect changes in the law. This only applied to C corporations.

Contribution of property. DOL No. 90-05A (March 29, 1990): A DOL Advisory Opinion allowed the contribution of property (buildings in this case) to an ESOP that would constitute 10.4% of plan assets.

Employer securities transferred to defined contribution plan of a subsidiary. (Private letter ruling, number unavailable): The IRS issued a private letter ruling on October 18, 2012, regarding the transfer of employer securities from the defined contribution plan at a parent company to a comparable plan established at a subsidiary during a corporate restructuring. The ruling stated that the shares of the parent corporation transferred to the defined contribution plan at the subsidiary "will be treated as 'securities of the employer corporation' for purposes of Code section 402(e)(4)" and that "the net unrealized appreciation in such shares may be excluded from gross income upon distribution to a participant or beneficiary on or before December 31, 2011, to the extent provided in Code section 402(e)(4)." Additionally, the ruling addressed whether the reinvestment restrictions placed on the subsidiary plan would cause the plan to violate the diversification requirements of Code Section 401(a)(35). The restrictions prevented participants of the new plan from investing new or existing account balances in the stock funds of the parent or subsidiary. Instead, participants were given the opportunity to voluntarily dispose of those shares during a time frame, and at the end of the time frame, the company would liquidate the stock funds. On this issue, the IRS found that after the spin-off, shares of the parent company no longer qualified as investments in employer securities and therefore were not subject to the diversification requirements. Furthermore, the stock fund of the subsidiary company "is a frozen fund within the meaning of Section 1.401(a) (35)-(e)(2)(vii)(A)," and therefore the restriction on reinvesting in the subsidiary company's shares is "not treated as an indirect restriction on Code section 401(a)(35) diversification rights."

Definition of Employer Securities

OTC shares. PLR 200052014: Ruled that stock traded in the Over the Counter Bulletin Board market does not qualify as a readily tradable security

Foreign company stock. PLR 200237026: Ruled that the shares of a foreign corporation's capital stock that were held in an ESOP trust maintained by a U.S. corporation that was wholly owned by the foreign corporation are "qualifying employer securities" under Sections 4975 and 409 of the Code and thus the company could potentially deduct dividends paid on the shares.

Foreign company stock. PLR 200205050: Ruled that a foreign corporation subject to tax under Section 881 of the Code can be treated as a member of a controlled group of corporations making it possible for employees of a U.S. subsidiary to be in an ESOP.

Discretionary funding triggers shares release. Chief Counsel Technical Advice Memorandum 200109010: The advice concludes that the Code Section 409(l) definition of qualifying employer securities is used to determine whether a plan qualifies as an ESOP, while the ERISA definition is used for prohibited transactions purposes. ERISA permits any class of stock to qualify as "qualifying employer securities," whereas Section 409(l) of the Code permits only certain common stock or convertible preferred stock to qualify as "qualifying employer securities." In this case, the trust did not actually purchase stock from the company. Instead, the company fixed a dollar amount to be contributed, then made a subsequent contribution in the form of stock to meet that dollar obligation. This discretionary funding approach could be construed to constitute a sale or exchange of property subject to the Code's prohibited transaction rules. The TAM declined to reach a conclusion on that.

In addition, the TAM allowed a prior determination letter to stand even though the plan language originally stated that any class of security could be in the ESOP. While the TAM said this was a prohibited transaction, it said that it would not overrule the prior letter of determination.

Pink sheet shares. PLR 9036039: Ruled that shares in a company that had been traded on the NASDAQ but then applied to be delisted and sold only on the pink sheets would be considered closely held for purposes of Section 1042. The IRS said that the term "readily tradable securities" meant publicly traded, not traded on pink sheets.

Convertible preferred stock. PLR 9836022: Ruled that convertible preferred stock received in a recapitalization immediately before a sale to an ESOP would qualify as common stock and thus be an eligible employer security under ESOP requirements. Moreover, the stock would not be "Section 306" stock subject to ordinary income taxation immediately upon the exchange.

Acquisition of nonqualifying shares. DOL Advisory Opinion 96-08A: Ruled that an ESOP's non-leveraged acquisition of a class of employer stock that did not constitute an "employer security" under Section 409(l) of the Code was exempt from the prohibited transaction rules.

NASDAQ stock. PLR 9529043: Ruled that common stock that was quoted on the NASDAQ SmallCap Market was "readily tradable" within the meaning of Code Section 409(l)(1).

Promissory notes. IRS Technical Advice Memorandum 9438002: Ruled that promissory notes issued for the payment of shares under an ESOP put option do not qualify as adequate security for the obligation and that more solid collateral (assets, insurance, etc.) is required.

Stock held by nonprofit. PLR 9421006: Ruled that a Section 501(c)(3) tax-exempt scientific research organization that held stock in a for-profit subsidiary could spin off that subsidiary, put the stock into an ESOP and 401(k) plan, and not lose its tax-exempt status.

New stock from reorganization. PLR 934036: Ruled that stock in employee accounts after a corporate reorganization would qualify as employer securities for treatment under net unrealized appreciation rules. The reorganization resulted in employees holding shares in the new company's stock as well as shares in the parent company that were transferred into the new ESOP.

IRS clarifies when valuations are needed for thinly traded ESOP companies. Notice 2011-19: This ruling, tilted "Definition of 'Readily Tradable' on an Established Security Market," put into regulations the long-held assumption that companies are considered privately held unless their stock is readily tradable on an established securities market. Pink sheet stock companies, therefore, would need an appraisal for their ESOP. Companies whose stock (or whose parent's stock) is traded on a foreign exchange, however, would not. Companies not defined as publicly traded now would be eligible for Section 1042 treatment for their owners.

Use of the Over-the-Counter Bulletin Board. PLR 201238031: In a private letter ruling issued on September 21, 2012, the IRS provided guidance on whether employer securities traded on the Over-the-Counter Bulletin Board (OTCBB) qualify as "publicly traded employer securities" under Section 401(a)(35)(G)(v) of the Code. The IRS ruled that the shares do not qualify as publicly traded, and therefore the company will not be considered to have publicly traded employer securities under Section 401(a)(35)(F).

Distribution Requirements, Procedures, and Taxation

Escrow accounts. PLR 200420036: The IRS confirmed that when an ESOP sells its stock and a portion of the purchase price is placed in escrow pursuant to an indemnification agreement or an earn-out, etc., the distribution to ESOP participants of certificates representing an interest in the escrow can be part of a valid rollover contribution to an IRA.

New interim DOL rules requiring companies with defined contribution plans, including ESOPs, to express a participant's benefit as an annuity (29 CFR Part 2520, Aug. 18, 2020).

(Chris Buch and Rafael Ramos Aguirre described the new rules in an NCEO newsletter article in 2020, reprinted below.)

Section 105 of the Employee Retirement Income Security Act of 1974 (ERISA), as amended, requires administrators of defined contribution plans to provide benefit statements on a periodic basis. The SECURE Act amended ERISA Section 105 to require benefit statements to include a statement of a participant's current account balance and an estimated lifetime stream of payments. This lifetime stream of payments is to be shown as both a single life annuity (SLA) and as a qualified joint and survivor annuity (QJSA). These changes will affect all defined contribution plans, including 401(k) plans and ESOPs.

The interim final regulations set forth the assumptions administrators must use to calculate a participant's retirement benefit and include model language that, if used, protects such administrators from liability that could arise in the event the calculations do not reflect the actual benefits a participant eventually receives.

Calculation of the benefit. The value of a participant's account balance is calculated as of the last day of the statement period. To calculate a participant's benefit, the interim final regulations provide assumptions that a plan administrator must follow. These assumptions include:

- Assumed commencement date: An administrator must calculate monthly payments as if such payments begin on the last day of the benefit statement period.
- Assumed age: An administrator must assume that the participant is the older of age 67 or the participant's actual age.
- Spouse and survivor assumptions: An administrator must assume the participant's spouse is the participant's same age regardless of the participant's marital status and must use a 100% QJSA.
- Assumed interest rate: An administrator must assume a rate of interest equal to the 10-year constant maturity Treasury securities yield rate for the first business day of the last month of the period to which the benefit statement relates.
- Assumed mortality: An administrator must use the unisex mortality table that is created and published by the Internal Revenue Service.

Special rules for in-plan annuities and deferred income annuities. The interim final regulations also provide guidance for plan administrators whose plans invest participants' accrued benefits in annuities through contracts with licensed insurance companies or who purchase deferred income annuities during the benefit accumulation phase. For those plans that offer in-plan distribution annuities, plan administrators will have the option of using the assumptions in the interim final regulations or the administrators may use the actual terms of the plan's insurance contract (subject to some limitations). There are separate disclosure requirements for those plans that offer deferred income annuities; however, any portion of an account that is not invested in a deferred income annuity needs to be disclosed according to the assumptions above.

Finally, the interim final regulations provide relief from ERISA liability for plan fiduciaries, sponsors, and others so long as the illustrations in the benefit statements meet the requirements of the interim final regulations. In addition to making the illustrations according to the interim final regulations, administrators must also include model language from the interim final regulations, or language that is substantially similar to the language in the interim final regulations in participants' benefit statements.

Effective date. The rules set forth in the interim final regulations will become effective one year from the publication date of the final rules. Final rules will be published after the comment period on the interim final regulations are closed and the DOL has had a chance to review all public comments.

Distribution Taxation

Net unrealized appreciation. PLR 200509032 and PLR 200507016: Allowed employees to take net unrealized appreciation (NUA) in cases where corporate transactions resulted either in employer securities in one company being replaced with employer securities in another or where employer contributions of stock were sold, followed by an employee election to invest in employer stock.

Net unrealized appreciation. PLR 199919039: Ruled that distributions from an ESOP after a complex reorganization were eligible for net unrealized appreciation treatment.

Net unrealized appreciation. PLR 199931051: Ruled that shares in an ESOP transferred to a company's former subsidiary are still treatable as qualifying employer securities for purposes of eligibility for net unrealized appreciation.

Net unrealized appreciation. PLR 199928034 and PLR 9721036: Ruled that a participant who elects to roll over the cash portion of an ESOP into an IRA and sell the shares outside of the IRA can take net unrealized appreciation on the sale of the shares

Averaging contribution bases. PLR 9147053: Ruled a company could use the average of the various bases for calculating the value of contributions to an ESOP for calculating net unrealized appreciation. The company, which had multiple subsidiaries, operated a KSOP with a complex system for using employee contributions, employer contributions, and earnings on shares to repay a loan.

IRS allows employees a second chance if they missed 60-day rollover requirement for an IRA. Rev. Proc. 2016-47: In Revenue Procedure 2016-47, the IRS established a self-certification process for an employee to get a second chance at a tax-deferred rollover from a retirement plan into an IRA. The taxpayer has to be able to show that an inadvertent error, such as a lost check, illness, confusion about whether the institution providing the IRA was qualified, or a variety of other circumstances caused the error. The taxpayer then has 30 days to correct it. The provider can accept the self-certification unless it has knowledge that it is incorrect. The IRS can, however, challenge the waiver on audit.

IRS Provides Guidance on Taxability of Floor Price Protection Plans: In General Legal Advice Memo 2019-03, the IRS ruled that payments from a company to a former employee under a price protection plan are immediately taxable if made directly to the employee, but not if the employer makes a special "qualified non-elective contribution" to the plan that is allocated to the former employee's account, and then distributed as part of the ultimate account distribution. Once those funds are distributed, they would be taxed under normal distribution rules.

Floor price protection plans are used by some non-100% ESOPs as part of a leveraged transaction to buy more shares. The new debt puts downward pressure on the stock price until the loan is repaid. Employees nearing retirement age can be adversely affected, so price protection plans allow companies to make up some or all the difference the added leverage creates. The vast majority of the plans do this by making an additional cash payment to employees covered by the plan (often those 55 or older) equal to this difference. There are different ways of computing this, but the goal is to assess what the stock price would have been absent the leverage and provide the employee with a total payout not less than that.

It is already the standard practice of ESOP companies to treat the direct payments to employees as taxable income.

Diversification

Eligibility. ESOP Cadre Guidance, November 2009: For purposes of diversification eligibility, an ESOP may use (1) "participant and former participant" instead of "employee" and (2) "year of service" instead of "year of participation," as long as the "year" in either case does not require more than 1,000 hours of service. A year of participation can also be defined as a year in which the individual has an account balance in the ESOP. A plan document may provide that a participant with at least 10 years of participation who terminates employment before reaching age 55 will become a qualified participant for diversification purposes upon reaching age 55 after termination of employment. The guidance indicates companies cannot change plans to make them more restrictive.

Eligibility. PLR 200234070: The IRS ruled that company stock previously held by an ESOP that was acquired before January 1, 1987, then transferred to a 401(k) plan in a corporate acquisition, will not be subject to the diversification rules of Section 401(a)(28)(C) of the Code. The plan acquired stock previously held by an ESOP. The ruling on the complex transaction also discussed how to calculate what the basis would be for calculating net unrealized appreciation for company stock.

Diversification rules in public companies. Notice 2013-17: The IRS granted relief for public companies that need to amend their plans because of conflicting diversification requirements. Under Section 401(a)(28), ESOP companies must provide diversification options for employees who have 10 years of service in the plan and are 55 or older. Some companies do that by making a distribution to employees. That distribution could be considered a cutback in benefits, but the IRS specifically exempted this procedure from anti-cutback rules. Effective in 2006, public companies have had a conflict, however, in that they have a very different set of diversification requirements under Section 401(a)(35) than they did under the Section 401(a)(28) rules that until then had applied to them. Companies that became public after adopting the procedure on making a distribution to satisfy the 401(a)(28) rules, or that have not amended their plans in light of the 401(a)(35) rules that apply to them, have to make amendments to the plan because the distribution option now is no longer is protected under the anti-cutback rules. In this notice, the IRS outlines procedures for making amendments retroactively to comply with this potential conflict.

Dividends

Reporting. IRS Announcement 2008-56 (June 30, 2008): Plans must report Section 404(k) dividends on one IRS Form 1099-R and report all other distributions on another IRS Form 1099-R.

Distributions as dividends. IRS Final Regulations Regarding Deductibility of Redemption of Employer Securities (71 Fed. Reg. 51471 [Aug. 30, 2006]): Bars companies from claiming deductions for the repurchase of distributed shares as allowable deductible dividends under Section 404(k).

Distributions as dividends. IRS REG-133578-05 (Aug. 25, 2005): States that deductions for qualifying dividends on ESOP shares must be taken at the parent company level, not the subsidiary. The ruling also addressed whether the parent or subsidiary was eligible for a 404(k) deduction.

Foreign securities. PLR 200237026: The IRS ruled that the shares of a foreign corporation's capital stock that were held in an ESOP trust maintained by a U.S. corporation that was wholly owned by the foreign corporation are "qualifying employer securities" under Sections 4975 and 409 of the Code and thus the company could potentially deduct dividends paid on the shares.

Dividend reinvestment. IRS Notice 2002-2: This provided guidance on requirements for dividend reinvestment in ESOP shares.

Among several issues, it provided that:

- Dividends reinvested in company stock are deductible in the later of the tax year in which the dividend is reinvested or the tax year in which the election becomes irrevocable.
- Participants must be given a "reasonable" opportunity to make the election before the dividend is paid or distributed; must be able to change their election at least annually; and, if there is an amendment affecting how dividends will be paid, participants must be able to reinvest before this tales effect.
- Dividends are not subject to annual addition limits.
- Any dividends that a participant elects to reinvest in company stock must be 100% vested.
- The reinvestment election may be made available to ESOP participants who are no longer employees, as well as to beneficiaries.

Dividend switchbacks. PLR 199921056: This is the last of several rulings (PLRs 9821064, 9825034, 199921056, PLR 9829042, 199938040, 9840048, 9841045, 9530006, 9526023, 9518018, 9321065, and 9442027) allowing the use of "dividend switchbacks" in ESOPs. The technique was used to allow companies to make it possible for employees to reinvest dividends in company stock in the plan on a pre-tax basis. The Economic Growth and Tax Relief Act of 2001 expanded Section 404(k) of the Code to obviate the need for this by providing statutory authority of the pre-tax reinvestment of dividends in company stock in an ESOP. In PLR 9321065, the IRS also ruled that neither the elective deferrals to the 401(k) plan nor the additional employer contributions to the 401(k) in the amount of the ESOP dividends would constitute wages subject to federal income tax withholding under Code Section 3402, because Code Section 3401(a)(12)(A) generally exempts from the definition of wages remuneration paid to, or on behalf of, an employee or his beneficiary from or to a Code Section 401(a) trust. However, these elective deferrals and additional employer contributions would constitute wages for purposes of FICA and FUTA.

401(k) conversion. PLR 199909058 and PLR 199915064: Both PLRs ruled that companies could not deduct dividends paid on company stock under Section 404(k) that was acquired in a 401(k) that was then converted to an ESOP.

Reorganization. TAM 199923047: Ruled that dividends paid in ESOP shares after a corporate reorganization were deductible. In this case, a company ("Target") spun off four of its existing businesses to a successor firm. This new company set up an ESOP and employees got one share in the new company for each ESOP share they had in Target. As part of the spin-off, the company declared a special dividend to shareholders, including the ESOP. The IRS ruled this special dividend was deductible, not taxable income pursuant to a reorganization.

Subsidiary employees. PLR 9850022: Ruled that dividends of parent company stock paid to ESOP plan participants who were employees of subsidiaries of the parent firms were deductible under Section 404(k).

Timing. PLR 9821064 and PLR 9825034: Ruled that employers could deduct dividends distributed to ESOP participant shares to the extent they were distributed within 90 days of the close of the plan year in which they were paid.

Distributions as dividends. IRS Technical Assistance Memorandum 9612001: Ruled companies cannot deduct costs of ESOP distributions as dividends under Section 404(k) of the Code.

Reasonableness. PLR 9522041: Ruled that a dividend paid on stock held by an ESOP that was in the upper range of the market rate for comparable publicly traded dividend paying securities was deductible under Code Section 404(k).

Reorganization. PLR 9514021: Ruled that stock in a newly created subsidiary held by an ESOP would continue to be qualifying employer securities after the parent merged with another company and, as part of the transaction, spun off all of its assets to the subsidiary and transferred the shares owned by the ESOP to this new company. The parent had used an ESOP to borrow money to buy its stock in the first place, and the issue now was whether dividends paid on the parent company stock that became shares of the spun-off company were still deductible after the transaction. The IRS ruled they would be.

Timing. PLR 9419031. Ruled that dividends passed through to employees within 90 days after the end of the plan year are deductible.

Reorganization. PLR 9430027: Ruled dividends paid on corporate stock in an ESOP after restructuring are deductible.

Reasonableness. PLR 9304003: Ruled that a dividend that was effectively at 66.67% of the value of the shares was not reasonable and thus not deductible. The company had used a 66.67 cents per share dividend rate when the share price was $10 per share, but after a redemption the number of shares was reduced to 10% of what it had been. Now the 66.67 cent per share dividend was worth 10 times as much per share, so the IRS ruled that their use to repay an ESOP loan was not deductible because the rate was not reasonable.

Money purchase plan. PLR 9134024: The IRS allowed a company with an ESOP and money purchase pension plan to use dividends to repay an ESOP loan.

Terminated plan. PLR 9011047: Ruled that payments to employees from a direct dividend account that consisted of assets from a terminated ESOP, including dividends on those shares, did not constitute a separate contribution under Code Section 72.

Eligibility, Vesting, and Allocation Issues

Reshuffling or rebalancing. ESOP Cadre Guidance (Feb. 2010): Advises that reshuffling or rebalancing of ESOP accounts is acceptable provided a number of requirements are met, including that there is a "definite written program" and a "definite predetermined allocation formula." The plan must state the manner in which the transfers will be accomplished. Previously diversified shares cannot be subject to reshuffling, rebalancing, or segregation. Segregated accounts must offer sufficient investment options to the participant.

Vesting. PLR 200929023: Ruled that a faster vesting schedule is not required in the case where three of four ESOP loans were refinanced after the Pension Protection Act's grandfathering date for new faster vesting rules because one grandfathered loan remained.

Vesting. IRS Notice 2007-7 (Jan. 29, 2007): Provides guidance and effective dates on new vesting rules under the Pension Protection Act of 2006, including requiring vesting be completed in no more than six years (for graded vesting) or two years (for cliff vesting). If there are shares acquired by an ESOP loan in effect as of September 26, 2005, they can be vested under the old rules.

LLCs and partnerships. PLR 200116051 and PLR 200111053: Ruled employees of an LLC that did not make an election to be taxed as a corporation and which is a subsidiary of a C corporation are eligible to participate in an ESOP.

LLCs and partnerships. PLR 200008040: Ruled that the employees of a partnership taxable as a corporation for federal tax purposes are eligible ESOP participants. The partnership was part of a complex set of ownership arrangements by a publicly traded parent.

LLCs and partnerships. PLR 199949046: Ruled that employees of five subsidiary LLC's that did not make an election to be taxed as a corporation and that are subsidiaries of a C corporation are eligible to participate in an ESOP. In this ruling, however, the IRS also allowed employees of another LLC subsidiary that did choose to be taxed as a corporation to participate in the ESOP, a different conclusion than other PLRs on partnerships and LLC's.

LLCs and partnerships. PLR 199916055: Ruled that employees of a partnership can participate in an ESOP of a parent C corporation when the partnership has filed an election to be taxed as a corporation.

Floor-offset plans. PLR 9543046: This very complex ruling dealt with a floor-offset arrangement for an ESOP. These plans were no longer allowed after December 17, 1987, so this complex ruling is only of historic interest.

Eligible payroll. PLR 9442015: Ruled that (1) compensation of employees who were ineligible to receive allocations of company stock because of the rules under Section 1042 of the Code would not count as eligible payroll for ESOP contribution limits and that (2) company stock received by certain key employees outside the ESOP pursuant to an incentive stock option plan, a non-qualified stock option plan, and a restricted stock plan would not violate the prohibited allocation rules of Code Section 409(n)(1), even after they owned more than 25% of any class of company stock or the total value of company stock.

ESOP/401(k) Plans

Diversification. IRS T.D. 9484 (June 14, 2010), Diversification Requirements for Certain Defined Contribution Plans: The Pension Protection Act required that plan participants in defined contribution plans in publicly traded companies other than stand-alone ESOPs must be allowed to diversify out of employer stock at any time for shares they bought with deferrals and after three years for shares bought by employer contributions. There must be at least three diversified options. The plan may limit the opportunities to reinvest to periodic reasonable periods, but not less than quarterly.

The regulations describe how control group companies would be defined under the law and specified certain exceptions, such as regulated investment company holdings, that would not be affected. Plans may not impose direct or indirect restrictions or conditions on the investment of employer securities that are not imposed on the investment of other plan assets other than to comply with securities laws. The regulations describe a number of specific exemptions to the impermissible restriction rule, such as complying with short-term trading requirements, certain tax consequences, etc.

Default investments. DOL Final Rule, Default Investment Alternatives Under Participant Directed Individual Account (29 CFR Part 2550, 2007): Spells out what default investment alternatives will be available in participant directed retirement plans (which would include a KSOP). Company stock is not one, but exceptions are made where the company's stock is held by a registered investment company or if company stock is acquired as matching contributions made by the plan sponsor or at the direction of a participant or beneficiary prior to management by an investment management service, provided that the investment management service has the discretion to dispose of (but not acquire additional) employer securities.

Testing requirements. IRS T.D. 9169 (Dec. 29, 2005) and IRS Internal Revenue Bulletin 2005-5: Final regulations in T.D. 9169, further elaborated in the IRS bulletin, made it easier for companies combining 401(k) plans and ESOPs to meet testing requirements by allowing the use of aggregate testing to see if the plans meet anti-discrimination requirements.

Federal Contractor Rules

Cost allowability. Cost Accounting Standards Board Final ESOP Reimbursement Regulations (73 Fed. Reg. 23961, May 1, 2008): Ruled that companies can be reimbursed for ESOP contributions based on the value of the shares at the time the contribution is made. For leveraged ESOPs, the allowability of the costs follows Federal Acquisition Regulation Part 31, meaning companies can charge the costs of principal and interest on an ESOP loan provided that the stock is acquired at fair market value. Dividends also are allowed as a cost.

Department of Defense Guidance Issued on Pilot ESOP Contract Preference Program (Nov. 8, 2022): The 2022 National Defense Authorization Act created a pilot program, known as Section 874, that allows the Department of Defense (DOD) to award certain follow-on contracts without initiating a competitive process to 100% ESOP-owned businesses that meet the definition of a "qualified business." The guidelines in this memo stated that "contracting officers supporting a program selected for participation in the pilot will be able to award a follow-on contract for the continued development, production, or provision of products or services that are the same or substantially similar to those procured by DOD under a previous contract with a 'qualified business' under the authority of § 3201(c)(5)." Contractor submissions will be accepted until April 28, 2023, or until the DOD approves nine contracts for award under the pilot program. A qualified business will be limited to a single opportunity for the award of a sole source follow-on contract. Not more than 50% of the amount paid under the follow-on contract may be expended on subcontracts.

Fiduciary Issues

Definition of fiduciary. DOL Proposed Regulation on Definition of the Term "Fiduciary" (Oct. 21, 2010): This controversial proposal redefined the term "fiduciary" for a variety of ERISA plan purposes, but specially also defined ESOP appraisers as fiduciaries. In 2016, in "Definition of the Term 'Fiduciary': Conflict of Interest Rule—Retirement Investment Advice," 29 CFR Parts 2509, 2510, and 2550, the DOL said that it would not consider ESOP appraisers as fiduciaries, but that it would start a special project on ESOP valuation requirements.

Department of Labor agreement with GreatBanc provides template for ESOP fiduciaries. On June 2, 2014, GreatBanc Trust Company and the Department of Labor entered into an "Agreement Concerning Fiduciary Engagements and Process Requirements for Employer Stock Transactions." In its press release, GreatBanc praised the agreement as "a product of constructive and collaborative discussions with top DOL officials in Washington D.C." and said "we are happy to have established a positive channel of communication with top decision makers in the DOL," and "we look forward to a positive relationship with the DOL going forward."

In the DOL's press release, Assistant Secretary of Labor for Employee Benefits Security Phyllis C. Borzi said that "others in the industry would do well to take notice of the protections put in place by this agreement. ESOPs are an important tool to promote employee ownership, not a way to create big cash-outs for owners and top executives."

The agreement sets forth a process to be followed when GreatBanc, as trustee, purchases or sells stock on behalf of an ESOP. In its press release, GreatBanc said that "in a series of meetings with the DOL officials, GreatBanc Trust informed them about the excellent policies and procedures that GreatBanc Trust has had in place for many years. The DOL contributed its ideas, and mutually agreed that it would be helpful to spell these out in a written document."

The agreement has several key elements, described below. The agreement is discussed in detail in the NCEO publication *The DOL Fiduciary Process Agreement for ESOP Transactions* (2014), coauthored by attorneys involved in negotiating the agreement.

Valuation Assessment

The trustee must "prudently investigate the valuation advisor's qualifications" and take "reasonable steps to determine that the valuation advisor receives complete, accurate and current information necessary to value the employer securities." It also must determine "that its reliance on the valuation advisor's advice is reasonable before entering into any transaction in reliance on the advice." The appraiser should not have valued the stock that is to be the subject of the transaction with the ESOP for a party to the transaction other than the trustee.

Trustees need to document why they chose the appraiser and how they vetted the appraiser's qualifications. This need not be done every time for appraisers used regularly. The trustee should know the qualifications of who is actually doing the work, not just the firm.

One of the more important parts of the agreement concerns the specific documentation a trustee should ask for from the appraiser. These include looking at a number of specific metrics on projected financial performance and how they compare over the prior five-year prior period as well as to comparable public company data, if any. The measurements described are fairly standard in good ESOP appraisals; the agreement specifies some what to look for and document.

The agreement also provides that the appraiser's report or trustee's documentation should demonstrate consideration of "how the plan document provisions regarding stock distributions, the duration of the ESOP loan, and the age and tenure of the ESOP participants, may affect the ESOP sponsor's prospective repurchase obligation, the prudence of the stock purchase, or the fair market value of the stock." This underscores an emerging, but not yet universal, practice to consider repurchase obligations and other distribution issues in connection with the appraisal.

The agreement requires that the trustee evaluate the debt for the transaction and how capable the company is of repaying it. It also requires that the trustee consider the fairness of the transaction with respect to such issues as whether the cost of the debt is reasonable.

The agreement states a clear preference for audited company financial statements in connection with the appraisal. If the company's financial statements are not audited, the trustee needs to document why is reasonable to rely on unaudited financial information.

Proving the Right Information to the Appraiser

The agreement provides that the trustee should document that any information, including financial projections, that are provided to the appraiser are reasonable. The trustee should also document that is has considered a list of 16 different items in the valuation report, including assumptions as to various discounts, adjustments to financial projections made by the appraiser, the weighting of various methods of appraisal, discount rates, treatment of debt, assessment of the company relative to markets and the industry, and other standard elements of ESOP appraisals.

The trustee also should document the specific steps taken to assess the valuation report as well as who did the work. That should include a discussion of the questions asked and areas of disagreement and how they were resolved.

The agreement also provides that "the Trustee will consider whether it is appropriate to request a claw-back arrangement or other purchase price adjustment(s) to protect the ESOP against the possibility of adverse consequences in the event of significant corporate events or changed circumstances. A "claw back" generally requires that the seller returns some of the price it received for stock it sold in the event that the value of the stock goes down significantly during a specific period of time after the transaction. It is difficult to get a seller to agree to such a provision, but the agreement states that "the Trustee will document in writing its consideration of the appropriateness of a claw-back or other purchase price adjustment(s)."

Department of Labor issues new guidance for voting company stock in retirement plans. In Interpretive Bulletin 2016-1, the Department of Labor issued new guidance for fiduciaries of retirement plans that have company stock as one of their investments. The guidelines are aimed at fiduciaries in public companies, but would be applicable to ESOPs as well, albeit in a limited way.

The DOL said it was concerned that the interpretations of prior guidance (in Interpretive Bulletins 94-2 and 2008-2) are "out of step with important domestic and international trends in investment management and have the potential to dissuade ERISA fiduciaries from exercising shareholder rights, including the voting of proxies, in areas that are increasingly being recognized as important to long-term shareholder value." This can include engagement on environmental and social goals.

The DOL said that fiduciaries can establish that "an investment policy that contemplates activities intended to monitor or influence the management of corporations…is likely to enhance the value of the plan's investment in the corporation, after taking into account the costs involved." Such activity could include such issues as "the independence and expertise of candidates for the corporation's board of directors and assuring that the board has sufficient information to carry out its responsibility to monitor management. Other issues…included such matters as consideration of the appropriateness of executive compensation, the corporation's policy regarding mergers and acquisitions, the extent of debt financing and capitalization, the nature of long-term business plans, the corporation's investment in training to develop its work force, other workplace practices and financial and non-financial measures of corporate performance." Any actions taken by fiduciaries, however, "may not increase expenses, sacrifice investment returns, or reduce the security of plan benefits in order to promote collateral goals."

The guidance does not draw a clearly defined line of when consideration of social and environmental goals is appropriate as a long-term strategy and when it is inappropriate, but it clearly does give fiduciaries more leeway to take an active role in pursuing these and other long-term corporate goals.

The application to private company ESOPs is limited. The guidance reiterates that the trustee must vote the shares unless a named fiduciary is directing the trustee or a named fiduciary delegated such power to one or more investment managers. It also makes very clear that ESOP trustees do need to take their role as shareholders seriously.

DOL Issues New Guidance on Proxy Voting in Retirement Plans: The issue of whether trustees can and should override participant directions on offers to buy shares in a proposed acquisition of an ESOP company has been one of the most ambiguous areas of ESOP law and practice. New guidance from the DOL (Financial Factors in Selecting Plan Investments, 85 FR 72846 [Nov. 13, 2020], 29 CFR 2550.404a-1) on proxy voting of shares in retirement plans, including on environmental, social, and governance (ESG) metrics, includes a brief section addressing this issue, essentially putting into regulatory form what had been just guidance. The new DOL guidance reaffirms that trustees "must not subordinate the interests of the participants and beneficiaries in their retirement income or financial benefits under the plan to any non-pecuniary objective, or promote non-pecuniary benefits or goals unrelated to these financial interests of the plan's participants and beneficiaries."

International ESOPs

Multinational company can include employees in ESOP. PLR 201510061: The IRS ruled that a multinational company with employees in multiple countries could include these employees in the ESOP and deduct contributions to the ESOP for them, provided they are (1) employed directly by the company and paid wages either directly by the company or through a payroll agency in the local jurisdiction, (2) employed by a disregarded limited liability corporation entity in the foreign country, or (3) paid by a local entity that is a foreign eligible entity that has elected to be a "disregarded entity."

Leveraged ESOP Issues

Allocation of suspense account shares on termination. ESOP Cadre Guidance (Nov. 2009): The use of proceeds from the sale of stock in a suspense account to pay for the ESOP loan is permitted only upon termination of the ESOP, at which time the plan document must be amended to provide for this.

Redemption. PLR 200733029: Ruled that the allocation of shares from a suspense account in an ESOP to repay an ESOP loan in a redemption would not be considered annual additions for purposes of Section 415 testing nor cause the ESOP loan to fail to meet the exempt loan requirements under Section 4975(d)(3) of the Code or the related Treasury Regulations (i.e., Treas. Reg. Section 54.4975-7).

The case involved a company that decided to terminate an ESOP for its subsidiary because of unanticipated business losses.

Allocation of suspense account shares on termination. PLR 200504040: Ruled that the allocation of shares from a suspense account in an ESOP to repay an ESOP loan in a redemption would not be considered annual additions for purposes of Section 415 testing nor cause the ESOP loan to fail to meet the exempt loan requirements under Section 4975(d)(3) of the Code or the related Treasury Regulations (i.e., Treas. Reg. Section 54.4975-7). Changes in the company's business made it unable to repay the loan, so it terminated the plan. The release of shares was insufficient to repay the loan, so the remainder would be forgiven.

Refinancing. DOL Field Assistance Bulletin 2002-1: This field assistance bulletin provides guidance to DOL officials in assessing whether ESOP loan refinancing is acceptable. In general, it states that ESOP loan refinancing is subject to the same prohibited transaction requirements as the original loan and must adhere to all the standard fiduciary obligations. The refinancing must be prudent and solely for the benefit of plan participants. For instance, extending a loan for too long could be an issue. The fiduciary might need to seek some benefit in return for refinancing, such as 1) assuring that shares held in the ESOP loan suspense account longer than they would have been under the terms of the original loan may not be sold and the proceeds used to repay the outstanding portion of the ESOP refinanced loan unless the ESOP is terminated and the proceeds are paid to participants; 2) providing a dividend make-whole provision to compensate for any potential lost dividends; 3) additional diversification rights; or 4) greater employer contributions.

Prepayment. PLR 200006054: Ruled that prepayment of an ESOP loan is not a violation of the primary benefit rule under ERISA.

Release of shares. PLR 200018058: In a ruling similar to the above PLR, the IRS ruled that the ESOP's sale of shares of company stock to the plan sponsor in connection with the termination of the plan pursuant to a merger did not violate the primary benefit rule or the requirement that an ESOP loan be for a specific period.

Allocation of suspense account shares on termination. PLR 200034039: The IRS ruled that the use of the proceeds from the sale of ESOP shares pursuant to a plan termination to repay a loan did not violate the exempt loan requirements of Section 4975(d)(3) of the Code. The IRS also ruled that any allocations pursuant to the sale would be considered earnings, not annual additions subject to the limitations of Section 415 of the Code. The use of this approach would also not change how the company calculates its deductions (which would be based on the dollars contributed to repay the loan).

Value of released shares. PLR 199929045: Ruled that a company could use the fair market value of shares released from a suspense account to calculate the value of annual additions under Section 415 of the Code. Most companies use the cost basis of the shares, which normally would be lower.

Release of shares. PLR 9837032: Ruled that a company using the proceeds from the sale of ESOP "suspense account" shares to repay ESOP loans would not cause the loans to fail the "primary benefit" requirement of Section 4975(d)(3)(A) of the Code.

Section 133. PLR 9847005: Ruled that the refinancing of an ESOP loan would not cause a loss of special tax treatment under former Code Section 133, which provided additional tax benefits for leveraged ESOPs meeting certain rules.

Allocation of suspense account shares on termination. PLR 9837032: First PLR ruling that the use of proceeds from the sale of stock in a suspense account pursuant to an acquisition were not considered annual additions for Section 415 purposes.

Section 133. PLRs 9722023,9314007, 9140066, and 9127020: Under the now expired Code Section 133 providing tax incentives for ESOP loans, qualifying securities had to be transferred to the ESOP within 30 days of when interest on the loan started to accrue. The IRS ruled this could be 30 days before or after.

Allocation of suspense account shares on termination. IRS Technical Assistance Memorandum (October, 1997, unpublished): As in PLR 200034039, ruled that the use of the proceeds from the sale of ESOP shares pursuant to a plan termination to repay a loan would not violate the exempt loan requirements of Section 4975(d)(3) of the Code. The IRS also ruled that any allocations pursuant to the sale would be considered earnings, not annual additions subject to the limitations of Section 415 of the Code. The use of this approach would also not change how the company calculates its deductions (which would be based on the dollars contributed to repay the loan).

Section 133. PLR 9736007: Ruled that the sale of stock from an ESOP that qualified under the now-defunct Section 133 within three years of their acquisition triggered a 10% excise tax.

Allocation of suspense account shares on termination. PLR 9648054 and PLR 9624002: Ruled that an ESOP's repayment of an exempt loan with part of the proceeds of its sale of unallocated stock to an acquiring company will not cause the loan to lose its exemption under Section 4975(d)(3) of the Code.

Allocation of suspense account shares on termination. PLR 9640027: Ruled that use of proceeds from the sale of stock in a suspense account to pay off an ESOP loan does not violate the primary benefit rule even though the purpose of the transaction was that the company determined the ESOP would provide an inadequate retirement benefit. This ruling is unique because the company's justification for the termination and repayment of the ESOP loan with suspense account shares was not the sale of the company but a retirement benefit decision.

Refinancing. PLR 9610028: Ruled that refinancing because the rising share price caused the value of shares released from the suspense account to increase substantially would not be a violation of the primary benefit rule. Many public companies leveraged ESOPs were designed as a match to 401(k) deferrals. If the stock price growth exceeded expectations, then more value was released than the company wanted to release. Refinancing slowed down this allocation.

Refinancing. PLR 9652024, PLR 9649050, and PLR 9648054: In all three cases, the IRS ruled that a refinancing of an ESOP loan to deal with a combination of an unexpected increase in shares price and an unexpected decrease in the number of participants would not violate the primary benefit rule of ERISA. As in PLR 9610028, the companies had anticipated released shares equal to a projected value needed to meet 401(k) deferrals, but that number was being substantially exceeded. In PLR 9648054, the IRS further ruled that the transaction, which was vetted by fiduciaries with a potential conflict of interest in the refinancing, did not constitute self-dealing.

Recapitalization. PLR 9626002: Ruled that dividends paid on two new classes of stock issued in a recapitalization of a corporation and held in an ESOP can be deducted if they otherwise meet the requirements of Section 404(k) of the Code.

Allocation of suspense account shares on termination. PLR 9621034: Ruled that the use of a portion of the ESOP suspense account shares to repay a portion of the ESOP debt, followed by the allocation of the excess shares and termination of that portion of the ESOP, would not violate the primary benefit rule. This was an unusual circumstance in which a company was selling a subsidiary. The acquirer would not retain the ESOP, so the portion of the stock attributable to the subsidiary could be sold to pay that portion of the debt, and the excess assets were distributed to those employees.

Refinancing. PLR 9530023: Ruled that the refinancing of an ESOP loan that would add 3.5 years to its term was not a violation of the primary benefit rule because the loan was needed to facilitate moving out of a high-crime area, the decrease in the annual contributions would only be from 12% to 8% of eligible pay, and the work force was young and stable.

Allocation of suspense account shares on termination. PLR 9507031: Ruled that terminating an ESOP for one of a controlled group of companies and using the sale proceeds to repay the loan was acceptable and that the allocations of the excess proceeds from the sale to employee accounts would not be treated as an annual addition.

Salary deferral to repay loan. IRS Technical Assistance Memorandum 9503002: Ruled that in an ESOP combined with a 401(k) plan, the use of salary deferral contributions as a source of repayment of the ESOP loan did not violate the exclusive benefit rule under Code Section 401(a)(2). The Department of Labor asked the IRS to reconsider that position, but the IRS did not make a change.

Loan write-down. PLR 9506030: Ruled that a write-down of an ESOP note pursuant to a bankruptcy reorganization would not be deductible, but the write-down would not cause the company's original loan to the ESOP to fail to qualify as an exempt loan under Code Section 4975(d)(3) because the "primary benefit requirement" was satisfied. Note that a write-down does not result in allocations to employee accounts; a normal loan forgiveness would and, most advisers believe, would be deductible just as a comparable contribution would be.

Refinancing. PLRs 9447057: Ruled that refinancing an ESOP loan to deal with unexpected financial problems did not violate the primary benefit rule of ERISA.

Refinancing. PLR 9437039 and 9443039: Ruled that refinancing an ESOP loan to deal with a significant reduction in the number of participants did not violate the primary benefit rule of ERISA.

Hostile acquisition. PLR 9431055: Ruled that a leveraged ESOP set up to prevent a hostile acquisition did not violate the primary benefit rule of ERISA (this is also listed under Mergers and Acquisitions).

Bad debt. PLR 9441017: Ruled that the repayment of an ESOP bank loan by former shareholders after the ESOP was unable to repay the loan was deductible as bad debt. The former owners had to sell their qualified replacement property to pay the loan.

Section 133. PLRs 9427011 and 9406009: Both rulings dealt with refinancing a loan under the now defunct Section 133 of the Code.

Allocation of suspense account shares on termination. PLRs 9416043, 9417032, 9417033, and 9426048: All dealt with the issue of whether proceeds from the sale of ESOP shares allocated to employee accounts would constitute annual additions. In these rulings, the IRS concluded they did, but in later rulings concluded they did not (see PLR 200733029 for the most recent ruling).

Redemption. PLR 9410025: Ruled that under Section 302(d) of the Code, the redemption of stock by a corporation from its ESOP to help repay an ESOP loan is treated as a distribution of property to the ESOP to which Section 301 of the Code applies, meaning it would be treated as dividends to the ESOP. It was not clear why this mattered, nor did the IRS address whether these dividends would then be deductible.

Share release. Technical Assistance Memorandum 201425019: The IRS ruled on a case where a company continued to release shares from an ESOP suspense account using the principal-only method even though a pledge agreement on a revised loan called for using the principal-and-interest method. The company's plan documents allowed shares to be released on a principal-only or principal-plus-interest method, but the original five-year loan called for the principal-only method. That loan was revised to ten years and called for an uneven amortization schedule. The new loan pledge agreement called for the principal-and-interest method, but the company continued to use the principal-only method. This not only violated the pledge terms but also violated the law's requirement that the principal-only method must be based on level amortization. In an agreement with the DOL, the company recalculated the allocations based on the principal-and-interest method and made retroactive corrections.

ESOPs and worker cooperatives now eligible for USDA loan guarantees. In Guaranteed Loanmaking and Servicing Regulations, 7 CFR Parts 4279 and 4287 (June 3, 2016), the Rural Business-Cooperative Service and Rural Utilities Service of the Department of Agriculture provided, for the first time, that loan guarantees may be made to ESOPs or worker cooperatives under the Business and Industry Guaranteed Loan Program. The maximum term is seven years. ESOP sellers cannot retain an interest more than five years. A rural area is "generally any area of a State other than a city or town that has a population of greater than 50,000 inhabitants and any urbanized area contiguous and adjacent to such a city or town." Guarantees are generally limited to $25 million.

SBA loans for ESOPs made easier. In Small Business Administration Procedural Notice 5000846607 (May 9, 2023), the Small Business Administration (SBA) took steps to make loans to ESOPs much easier than under prior rules. The agency had received considerable criticism for issuing requirements for ESOP loans that are inconsistent with the language and intention of the Main Street Employee Ownership Act (MSEOA). That law was passed in 2018 to remove numerous barriers that made SBA loans or loan guarantees for ESOP acquisitions impractical. The law was also designed to allow ESOPs to qualify for loans under the SBA's 7(a) program, which allows qualified lenders to process loan applications that can receive SBA guarantees. The loans can be for up to $5 million. The law stipulated that the SBA's administrator "may" make the changes the law provided, but the regulations SBA initially issued made things harder, not easier.

The SBA had required that there be an equity infusion of at least 10% when an ESOP bought a company; that ESOP loans could not go through the SBA's 7(a) program, which allows participating banks to make SBA-guaranteed loans directly to borrowers instead of their having to go through the SBA; that owners had to make a personal loan guarantee when the ESOP was buying a controlling interest; and that there to be a valuation for the SBA in addition to the ERISA-required valuation. Procedural Notice 5000846607 both dropped the equity requirement and limited the personal loan guarantee requirement to situations in which the ESOP owns less than 100% of the company.

In its Small Business Administration Affiliation and Lending Criteria (13 CFR 120 and 13 CFR 121, April 10, 2023, the SBA changed its rule that ESOP loans be made only by the SBA, not through the 7(a) participating lender program. The same guidance indicates that there does not need to be a separate valuation for the SBA, as has often been required in the past. The guidance language does not specifically state this, but the requirements for the valuation would seemingly be met by a valuation done under ERISA standards. 7(a) lenders can make this determination themselves.

Limited Liability Companies

Limited liability companies taxed as corporations can have ESOPs. In Private Letter Ruling 201538021, the IRS allowed limited liability companies (LLCs) to adopt an ESOP under certain circumstances. The PLR clarifies that unit shares of a limited liability company that is classified as an association and that has elected to be taxed as a corporation are "employer securities" as defined in the Code, provided that they have the same rights to distributions, dividends, and liquidation proceeds. Under prior rules in the LLC that was the subject of this PLR, some unit shares had different voting rights, but this will be amended so they all have the same rights. The IRS ruled that because the company has no common shares meeting the ordinary definition of eligible securities, its unit shares will qualify for this purpose.

Mergers and Reorganizations

Tax-free exchange. PLR 200017034: The IRS ruled that an exchange of common stock for an ESOP stock would be treated as a tax-free Section 368 exchange and not as a distribution of property under Section 301 of the Code.

ESOP company acquisition of target company. PLR 200052023: In PLR 200052023, the IRS ruled that an acquisition of all of the outstanding stock of an unrelated target corporation in an exchange for stock of the acquiring corporation with an ESOP was a valid tax-free reorganization. See also under Section 1042 for 1042 implications.

Spin-off. PLR 199923027: Ruled that an ESOP set up to hold stock whose performance would be directly linked to the company's performance would support the requirement under Code Section 355 that a spin-off be performed for a valid business purpose.

Tax-free exchange. PLR 9737020 and PLR 9738012: Ruled that complex restructurings involving an ESOP in public companies were tax-free reorganizations.

Profit-sharing plan merger. PLR 9720037: Ruled that the merger of a profit sharing plan into an ESOP satisfied the requirements of Section 414(l) of the Code and Treas. Reg. Section 1.414(l)-1(d). The ESOP leveraged share suspense account must be preserved in the merger.

Spin-off. Revenue Procedure 96-30, 9649042, 9617022, and PLR 9538013: Ruled that establishing an ESOP in a subsidiary is a valid business purpose so that the spin-off is in accordance with the requirements of Section 355 of the Code.

Spin-off. PLR 9643033: Ruled on a complex transaction involving a spin-off of a subsidiary involving an ESOP. The PLR provides a detailed checklist of issues a company should comply with to assure the transaction is in accordance with Section 355 of the Code.

Net operating losses. PLR 9510007: Ruled that ESOP plan participants are treated as owners of stock for purposes of Section 382 of the Code (which concerns limits on net operating loss carryforwards following certain changes in ownership), and therefore past distributions of company stock from an ESOP do not constitute owner shifts or equity structure shifts for purposes of determining whether an ownership change has taken place. Section 382 of the Code provides for a limitation on net operating loss carryforwards following certain changes in ownership of a corporation.

Hostile acquisitions. PLR 9431055: Ruled that a leveraged ESOP set up to prevent a hostile acquisition did not violate the primary benefit rule of ERISA (this is also listed under Leveraged ESOPs). This appears to be the only IRS ruling on this issue.

Spin-off. PLR 9411038: This PLR concerned an extremely complex transaction in a public ESOP company, concluding a subsidiary spun off from the parent can sell the stock in the parent ESOP it received in the transactions but cannot use the proceeds to buy anything other than the new sponsor's stock.

Spin-off. PLR 9314009: Ruled that the sale of a subsidiary and termination of its ESOP did not trigger taxation under Section 355 of the Code.

Spin-off. PLR 914902: Ruled that the spinoff of a subsidiary in a public company in a complex transaction could be accomplished so that subsidiary ended up with ESOP.

401(k)/ESOP merger. PLR 9124038: Ruled that where the parent company and a company it acquired both had KSOPs and the target's plan had assets from a former tax credit ESOP, the company could deduct dividends on all the shares in the merged plans.

Termination not change of ownership. PLR 9122060: Ruled that the termination of an ESOP and subsequent distribution of stock to participants did not constitute a change of ownership in a merger transaction.

Treatment of reorganization. PLR 202210004 (March 11, 2022): The IRS issued a private letter ruling concerning a complex business reorganization of a public company that offered an ESOP. The company spun off some of its assets to a new company it controlled and spun out another company as a separate entity. The company's ESOP now will include stock in both the parent and the controlled subsidiary. The IRS ruled the shares of the subsidiary held by the ESOP were qualifying securities and the basis for the shares in each plan would be determined by allocating the basis between the two plans based on their relative fair market value after the spinoff. Participants in the new controlled entity were also allowed to divest out of company stock into a new plan. The IRS ruled that this conversion would not be treated as a taxable event. The net unrealized appreciation on the sale would be made without regard to any temporary investment of company B stock sales proceeds.

PAYSOPs (Payroll-Based Stock Ownership Plans)

PLR 9025083: Complex ruling that dealt with how to aggregate a stock bonus plan with an ESOP feature, a profit sharing plan, and a terminated PAYSOP. Under current law, these aggregation issues are no longer relevant.

Plan Administration

Provider fees. DOL Interim Final Regulations for Plan Service Providers (July 16, 2010): These regulations detail how plan provider fees must be disclosed to plan fiduciaries. The target was primarily excessive fees in connection with 401(k) plans, but in ESOPs, it applies to plan fiduciaries, fiduciaries to an investment vehicle, registered investment advisors directly serving the plan, recordkeepers, and brokers of a self-directed plan if one or more investment alternatives are provided in connection with the recordkeeping or brokerage services are included. Few ESOPs would be covered by this last requirement because there are no participant-directed investments. In ESOPs, attorneys, accountants, auditors, valuation firms, and similar consultants are very unlikely to be covered by these rules unless they are getting income indirectly under one of the covered categories.

Contribution accounting. ESOP Cadre Guidance (Nov. 2009): A contribution to an ESOP followed by a payment on an exempt loan by the ESOP may not be done as a cashless transaction.

IRS Form 8955-SSA (Annual Registration Statement Identifying Separated Participants with Deferred Vested Benefits). In 2011, the IRS replaced Schedule SSA of the IRS Form 5500 annual report. Section 6057(a) of the Code, which requires plan administrators of retirement plans to file reports to provide information regarding certain separated participants with deferred vested benefits who have not commenced distributions. In addition to the IRS filing, affected participants must be provided an individual statement of the information reported, although this is usually satisfied with a benefit statement.

User fee increases. Revenue Procedure 2011-8: This ruling increased many user fees, including those required to file for determination letters.

IRS will no longer rule on coverage and nondiscrimination issues in determination letter process. Announcement 2011-82: The IRS will no longer rule on coverage and nondiscrimination demonstrations submitted as part of the determination letter process. Until this announcement, a plan sponsor could submit a "Schedule Q - Elective Determination Requests" with its determination letter to address these issues. The IRS will continue to review whether a plan's benefit and contribution formula satisfies the nondiscriminatory design-based safe harbors and 401(k) rules.

Voluntary compliance program. On January 13, 2013, the Department of Labor announced in a news release various changes in the Form 5500 delinquent filer voluntary compliance program. The changes include a requirement to file electronically, specified which forms need to be filed, and created an online calculator for penalties. For details, go to the Department's website at http://www.dol.gov/ebsa/newsroom/2013/EBSA012813.html.

IRS allows prototype ESOPs; drops determination letter requirement for periodic compliance. Looking to reduce its costs, the IRS plans to stop issuing determination letters for periodic compliance for ESOPs and other retirement plans. It also, for the first time, will allow prototype and volume submitter ESOP plan documents. The IRS has also issued sample plan language for ESOPs.

In Revenue Procedure 2015-36, the IRS included ESOPs meeting certain requirements in the plans qualifying for preapproval for initial and cyclical letters of determination if they adopt a prototype plan or volume submitter plan. Under a prototype plan, an employer can adopt a plan from a "sponsor" (here meaning the sponsor of the prototype, not the ESOP company) that is preapproved, or can use a plan submitted by a volume submitter (in the ESOP case, generally a law firm that submits a standard plan for multiple clients). The number of adopting employers for the same plan in either case must be at least 15, or 30 if the volume provider has multiple basic plan documents the clients use. Under this system, every preapproved plan must be submitted to the IRS for a new opinion or advisory letter every six years (rather than five for individual plans) during the applicable on-cycle submission period. A principal benefit of the plan is that providers and plan sponsors will be able to fit their plans into the six-year cycle for preapproved plans and would not need to vary language based on the latest cumulative list.

In that same revenue procedure, the IRS issued what it calls required modifications to plan documents seeking approval under the new procedure, although they are more accurately described as sample plan provisions.

ESOPs that are a part of a money purchase pension plan (which is now rare) or that use preferred stock cannot participate in this program. The ruling also sets out specific requirements the plan must include, all of which would currently be included in any well-drafted individual plan, such as rules for diversification, independent appraisal, diversification, meeting S corporation ESOP anti-abuse rules, etc. It also makes clear that the plan eligibility is limited to employees of the sponsor company and its controlled groups. Companies can make minor modifications of the plan and, probably, different allowable options for allocation, vesting, eligibility, and similar rules, although the ruling does not specifically say that.

IRS issues modified procedures for preapproved plans. Rev. Proc. 2017-41: On June 30, 2017, the IRS released Revenue Procedure 2017-14, which lays out revised procedures for obtaining opinion letters for preapproved plans, including ESOPs. Currently, an ESOP is available to plan sponsors only in the form of an "individually designed plan" that is submitted to the IRS for an individual favorable determination letter. Under the new program, document providers (such as law firms and other practitioners) may submit an ESOP document to the IRS for an opinion letter that "preapproves" the qualified status of the plan document. Document providers may submit an ESOP document to the IRS between October 2, 2017, and October 1, 2018. The IRS estimates the preapproval process to take about two years, and as a result, it will likely be a few years before document providers are able to offer preapproved ESOP documents to plan sponsors.

Revenue Procedure 2017-14 includes various changes to the submission process. It modifies prior rules by combining the programs for master and prototype (M&P) and volume submitter (VS) programs into a single new opinion letter program. Under the new program, a preapproved plan can be adopted as either a "standardized" or "nonstandardized" plan. Standardized plans follow more restrictive guidelines than nonstandardized plans.

Standardized plans must have certain provisions, most notably including that allocations be based on compensation. Nonstandardized plans can choose from more options in terms of plan design. Standardized plans are not available for stock bonus plans other than ESOPs, combined ESOP/money purchase plans (a rarity these days), or ESOPs that can hold preferred stock. A nonstandardized ESOP may include a Section 401(k) feature. Nonstandardized plans may also be customized, within certain IRS limits, without losing their "preapproved" status. It is likely that most preapproved ESOPs will be submitted as nonstandardized plans to provide for the greatest flexibility in plan design.

The new rules also follow up on prior rules issued in Revenue Procedure 2016-37. Among other things, these rules provided that every preapproved plan has a regular, six-year remedial amendment cycle. As a result, document providers must apply for new opinion letter once every five to six years. Plan sponsors will be required to adopt an updated version of the preapproved plan during each cycle. Since an individually designed plan is currently permitted to apply for IRS approval only upon adoption or termination of the plan, many view this ability to obtain IRS approval on a regular interval as a more favorable alternative.

It remains unclear whether ESOP plan sponsors will significantly move toward adopting preapproved plans or continue with individually designed plans. This determination will require further review and analysis based on IRS guidance provided, the provisions approved by the IRS in the preapproval process, and the unique terms of an existing plan.

IRS expands self-correction program. In Revenue Procedure 2019-19, the IRS expanded the Employee Plans Compliance Resolution System (EPCRS) to add additional failures that can be self-corrected. The EPCRS "permits any size business or organization that sponsors a retirement plan (including SEP and SIMPLE IRA plans) to identify and correct many failures they find." The new rules focus on correcting certain plan document failures, such as including participation requirements that are not allowed. Corrections must occur within two years. A second area concerns correcting plan loan features, something few ESOPs provide. The third area is the ability to correct certain operational failures, generally provided that they result in an increase in participation benefits and are allowable under ERISA. The rules also would make it easier to correct spousal consent errors in qualified domestic relations orders. The 125-page document provides details and examples.

DOL issues proposed ruling on electronic ERISA notifications: On October 3, 2019, the Department of Labor issued proposed new rules on filing electronic notices (84 FR 56894). The liberalized rule allows employers to have electronic notifications as the default method of delivery but allows employees to opt out and continue to receive paper notifications.

IRS Reiterates That Timely, Signed Documents Are Required for Plan Qualification: Reacting to the *Val Lanes* case (*Val Lanes Recreation Center v. Commissioner*, Docket No. 24887-10R [T.C. 2018-92, June 26, 2019]), a case in which a seemingly clearly abusive S corporation ESOP was allowed by a tax court, the IRS subsequently issued a General Legal Advice Memorandum (AM-2019-02, Dec. 13, 2019) stating employers should not rely on the *Val Lanes* rulings and should have a procedure by which plan changes and other required filings are properly and timely adopted, signed, and filed. The plan must be available to employees to inspect. The ruling said the Val Lanes case was unusual because the petitioner could claim that it had a pattern of issuing the signed documents but that flood damage provided a credible argument that it had done so, even though it could not produce the actual documents.

DOL Cybersecurity Guidance Issued: On April 14, 2021, the DOL issued a cybersecurity guidance package for ERISA plan sponsors. This is the DOL's first guidance directly addressing cybersecurity. The guidance includes three separate documents, linked below:

- Tips for Hiring a Service Provider with Strong Cybersecurity Practices
- Cybersecurity Program Best Practices
- Online Security Tips

The guidance is not regulatory but establishes what appear to be minimum standards expected by the DOL. The DOL makes it clear that plan fiduciaries need to mitigate cybersecurity risk. Risk mitigation can include such areas as electronic notifications, choosing plan providers and platforms, and tips on hiring cybersecurity contractors. There is additional guidance for recordkeepers.

ESOPs added to IRS volume adopter letter of determination program: In Revenue Procedure 2021-4, the IRS added ESOPs to Form 5307, the form used to submit letter-of-determination requests.

Under the rules,

> ESOP applications submitted on the current Form 5307 should be completed as follows:
>
> - Question 5a should be marked "6" – profit sharing plan,
> - The cover letter should state:
>   - That the submission is for an ESOP,
>   - whether the plan sponsor is a S or C corporation, and
>   - whether there was a change to the corporate status (from S to C or C to S revocation/election). If so, the cover letter should provide the effective date of such change.

IRS Issues New Guidance to Voluntary Correction Program: Revenue Procedure 2021-30 lays out a number of changes to the Voluntary Correction Procedure process for the correction of plan qualification errors. The new procedures generally will make it easier to use the process. Some of the changes affect only 401(k) plans, but others affect ESOPs as well.

When a company makes errors in its plan design or operations that could cause the plan to become disqualified, such as not making distributions on time or not crediting a qualified employee properly for a year of service, companies may be able to correct the error voluntarily. The Self-Correction Program (SCP) does not require filing with the IRS, and corrections can be made at any time. Whether an error is eligible for self-correction depends on the type and severity of the problem. The Audit Closing Agreement Program (Audit CAP) is used when the IRS finds an error. The Voluntary Correction Program (VCP) is used when the company needs to file its compliance actions with the IRS. Under prior rules, the self-correction time limit for errors that do not qualify as insignificant was two years. The new rules extend the limit to three years.

A second change concerns retroactive changes to plan documents. Plan sponsors were able to make retroactive changes to documents only if the changes improved benefit rights or plan features for participants, the change was permitted under IRS rules, and the benefit or feature improvement was available to all employees. Meeting all three criteria proved to be a difficult test because some changes were designed to fix a problem that applied only to certain employees. The new procedures eliminate the all-employees test.

A third change allows participants who receive an overpayment of benefits to repay them in a lump sum or installments.

Finally, the new rules end the ability of a plan sponsor to get feedback anonymously on proposed plan changes or corrections under voluntary correction programs before they are made. While this process has always been time-consuming and uncertain, from January 1, 2022, feedback can only be given at the IRS's discretion. Companies may not consider this to be a useful option.

EPCRS guidance. SECURE 2.0 expanded the application of the Employee Plans Compliance Resolution System (EPCRS), which allows companies to voluntarily correct certain errors. The current guidance on how to use the system is in Revenue Procedure 2021-30. SECURE 2.0 required that the IRS develop new guidance within two years of the date of the bill's enactment. In IRS Notice 2023-43 (May 23, 2023), the IRS issued advance guidance on the new provision that companies can use (pending the final rules) and also solicited comments on the proposal.

CARES Act and Disaster Act provisions. In IRS Notice 2022-45 (Nov. 7, 2022), the IRS extended plan amendment deadlines for compliance with Section 2022 of the CARES Act, which provided for COVID-related distributions, increased loan amounts, and delayed loan repayments, and with Section 302 of the Disaster Act, which provided favorable tax treatment for certain disaster-related loans or distributions. Amendments for these CARES Act and Disaster Act provisions had been required by the end of the 2022 plan year. The notice also clarifies that CARES Act and Disaster Act amendments adopted before the new December 31, 2025, deadline will not cause the plan to fail to satisfy anti-cutback requirements.

Change in Form 5500 participant count methodology affects which employee benefit plans will require an audit for 2023. In two Federal Register notices, Document #2023-02653 for the Notice of Final Forms Revision and Document #2023-02652 for Notice of Final Rulemaking (Feb. 23, 2023), the Department of Labor, IRS, and Pension Benefit Guarantee Corporation announced changes to the 2023 Form 5500 and Form 5500-SF Short Form that are intended to reduce overall filing costs for companies. The changes are effective for plan years beginning on or after January 1, 2023. A particularly significant change affects how the number of participants at the beginning of a plan year is counted, which in turn affects whether an audit by an independent accountant is necessary. This change reduces the time and fees incurred by the plan sponsor if the ESOP moves from a large plan (requiring an audit) to a small plan (not requiring an audit). Historically, independent plan audits have been required for benefit plans with 100 or more eligible participants on the first day of the plan year. For the 2023 Form 5500, the requirement for an independent audit will be based on the number of account balances and not the number of eligible employees. (The 80–120 exception rule still applies even with the new definition.) This change will be a relief for companies that sponsor an ESOP where employees meet the eligibility requirements to enter the plan, but fewer employees meet the allocation requirements to receive shares in the plan.

Plan-to-Plan Transfers

PLR 9004039: Ruled trustee-to-trustee transfers from a stock bonus plan and tax credit ESOP into a successor defined contribution plan resulted in tacking of years of active participation.

PLR 90350787: Ruled trustee-to-trustee transfers of defined benefit and PAYSOP accounts to an ESOP resulted in tacking of years of active participation.

Pension Plan Reversions

Surplus pension plan assets. PLR 9419030: Ruled that surplus assets from a defined benefit plan that were transferred to an ESOP would constitute employer securities after the company merged into another company. The stock in the ESOP was exchanged for stock in the acquiring company, which maintained the ESOP. The IRS also ruled that any remaining shares in the original company would not qualify.

Extension of time to purchase shares. PLR 9004019: Granted an extension of the 30-day period to acquire company stock with the proceeds from excess assets from a terminated defined pension plan.

Dividends in plan reversion. PLR 39810: Ruled that dividends on shares in an ESOP suspense account that were there as a result of a pension plan reversion and could not yet be allocated because of Section 415 rules could be used to pay off an ESOP loan, with resulting shares then adding to employee accounts.

S Corporation ESOP Anti-Abuse Rules

Reshuffling. Response to Technical Assistance Request #5 ("Memo #5") IRS (October 8, 2010): This response addressed the issue of whether an ESOP "reshuffling provision" (buying and selling shares between accounts in an ESOP) designed to prevent a nonallocation year under Code § 409(p)(3) would violate nondiscrimination testing rules. The approach would be used to prevent a participant from becoming a disqualified person by virtue of excess ownership in the ESOP. The response concluded that the reshuffling is likely to violate applicable regulations.

Transferring stock out of accounts. IRS Revised 409(p) Sample Language Regarding Transfers (originally issued in 2009 and updated since then, available at https://www.irs.gov/retirement-plans/sample-plan-language-for-section-409p-transfers): Sample language on how to transfer stock out of a potentially disqualified person's account into another plan to avoid a nonallocation year.

Transferring stock out of accounts. ESOP Cadre Guidance, November 2009: Said that discretionary provisions to allow the immediate buy back of stock from former ESOP participants would violate nondiscrimination provisions. Also provided that incorporation by reference of the provisions of Code Section 409(p) will be considered sufficient to constitute a "good faith" amendment until the end of the

EGTRRA remedial amendment period (the applicable cycle filing due date). As part of the determination letter process, however, S corporation ESOPs will be required to be amended to include additional "required language" spelling out what cannot be done. A participation waiver to avoid a nonallocation year must made before the beginning of the plan year and is irrevocable.

Family attribution rules. PLR 200804023: Ruled that the family attribution rules under IRC Section 318(a) regarding constructive ownership of stock do not apply for purposes of determining a 409(p) disqualified person.

Final anti-abuse regulations. IRS Final Regulations, Prohibited Allocations of Securities in an S Corporation (26 CFR Part 1, 2006): These regulations covered several issues:

- Violating the anti-abuse ("409(p)" rules constitutes a plan disqualification)
- A 409(p) violation can be avoided if an ESOP transfers sufficient shares to a non-ESOP portion of the plan, which must be "effectuated by an affirmative action taken no later than the date of the transfer." Shares held in the non-ESOP portion would be subject to unrelated business income tax.
- Targeted reshuffling of account balances in an ESOP to move shares out of potentially disqualified persons' accounts (but not to reshuffle all accounts on a non-discriminatory basis) is not an acceptable way to avoid a nonallocation year. People could, however, opt out of allocations in a year.
- Spells out other ways to avoid a nonallocation year, most notably selling or forfeiting synthetic equity and selling shares held outside the ESOP.
- Family attributions rules are spelled out in detail.
- A right of first refusal does not constitute synthetic equity.
- Clarifies that the IRS looks at accruals to a participant's account, not simply annual allocations, in determining a nonallocation year.
- Deemed distributions under a nonallocation year are not permissible rollover distributions.
- Spells out the complex rules for how to calculate the number of shares constituted by synthetic equity.

The regulations also included the rules set out in the temporary regulations described below in IRS Temporary Regulations 1.409(p)-IT.

Anti-abuse regulations. IRS Temporary Regulations 1.409(p)-1T "Prohibited Allocation of Securities in an S Corporation" (2004): These comprehensive rules were designed to prevent the abuse of ESOPs in S corporations. Penalties will now apply both to impermissible allocations and impermissible accruals. Stock in an individual's account, proceeds from the sale of stock, and distributions all are included in this definition. Plans can no longer avoid penalties by stipulating that individuals who accrue allocations in excess of the maximums specified in the law do not receive an allocation that year.

An individual is treated as owning outstanding non-ESOP stock if that individual has a right to acquire such stock *unless* the actual owner is: 1) subject to federal income tax; 2) the right is not one that would constitute a second class of stock; and 3) a principal purpose of the right is not to avoid taxation under the S ESOP rules. Second, for purposes of determining whose ownership makes them a disqualified person, the rules clarify that if any share is treated as owned by more than one person, then the share is counted as a single share, not a share separately owned by multiple people.

The new regulations require evaluating synthetic equity person-by-person so that the synthetic equity of other individuals does not count toward total share calculations for determining if that individual is a disqualified person.

The regulations added new wrinkles in determining what synthetic equity is. First, a nonqualified deferred compensation plan taken into account before January 1, 2005, for FICA purposes, that was outstanding on the first date the ESOP acquired shares, is now excluded. The second development was that the definition of synthetic equity, was expanded to include the right to acquire stock or assets in any related entity, not just the previously narrowly defined situations. The rules apply now to any rights to acquire assets in such an entity, not just goods, property, or services. The rights are calculated pro-rata to the S corporation's ownership interests in that entity. Third, for purposes of determining the total outstanding shares and individual ownership, the regulations count the right to acquire one share, through an instrument such as an option or restricted stock, as ownership of one share. For example, an option on 100 shares is treated as ownership of 100 shares. But the new regulations specify that a stock appreciation right has a value equal to the appreciation at the time of measurement, determined without regard to when the restrictions lapse. Presumably, a company would use some kind of valuation formula to assess this.

Another new rule provided that shares with voting rights greater than those in the ESOP are counted based on their voting rights. To ease this test, a company can use a moving three-year valuation, with new grants being adjusted at the next determination date.

Finally, in an important change, the rules provide that if an ESOP owns less than 100% of the stock, the synthetic equity calculations are done pro-rata to the ESOP's ownership. Thus, if the ESOP owns 30% of the shares, the synthetic equity interest would be multiplied by 0.3.

Anti-abuse settlements. IRS Announcement 2005-80 (2005): Sets out settlement procedures for improper S transactions.

Abusive transaction structures. IRS Revenue Ruling 2004-4: This comprehensive ruling shut down a number of abusive S ESOP transaction structures, including setting up qualifying subsidiaries, management corporations, etc.

Abusive transaction structures. IRS Revenue Ruling 2003-6: Addressed and prohibited abusive S ESOP corporation structures, including setting up shell corporations, as a means to avoid taxes. More important, it stated that transactions similarly lacking in business substance would be considered "listed transactions."

Plan language to prevent nonallocation year. PLR 201747007: A company asked the IRS about three possible approaches to prevent a nonallocation year in an ESOP:

1. If a company that had transferred ESOP assets to a non-ESOP plan or a separate portion of the ESOP then transferred those assets back to the ESOP, does that avoid creating a nonallocation year under Section 409(p)? (The assets were initially transferred to prevent a nonallocation year)
2. Can plan language exclude highly compensated employees who would be disqualified persons and use these allocations to distribute to non-highly compensated employees who are not disqualified persons?
3. Can plan language provide for multiple allocations of stock initially released to highly compensated employees until the percentage of pay released to highly compensated employees is the same as for non-highly compensated employees?

The IRS said the method in the first request could not be used because it would increase the change of a 409(p) violation and would likely violate coverage standards because the non-ESOP portion would likely only cover highly compensated employees.

IRS "issue snapshot" on Internal Revenue Code Section 409(p). On April 18, 2019, the IRS released an "issue snapshot," "Preventing the Occurrence of a Nonallocation Year Under Section 409(p)." Code Section 409(p) is designed to prevent the benefits of an ESOP in an S corporation from being too highly concentrated. The issue snapshot provides no new guidance but does provide an easy-to-follow explanation of Chief Counsel Advice (CCA) Memorandum 201747007 (Sept. 14, 2017), which set out the IRS's position on various ways to prevent a nonallocation year in an S corporation ESOP, such as transferring stock out of accounts of participants who might otherwise be deemed "disqualified persons" or excluding allocations to certain highly compensated employees. If people who fall under the definition of a "disqualified person" own (as defined by the 409(p) rules) 50% or more of the shares of an S corporation with an ESOP, the IRS deems this a nonallocation year, and the tax penalties for this are draconian.

S Corporation Issues Other Than Anti-Abuse Rules

Floor price agreements. PLR 200914019 and PLR 200827008: The IRS confirmed its position that an S corporation ESOP sponsor may provide a guaranteed or floor price arrangement for ESOP participants without violating the "one class of stock" restriction generally applicable to S corporations.

Temporary ownership of shares. IRS Revenue Procedure 2003-23. Provided that the temporary holding of company stock by an IRA trust established to roll over a distribution does not violate S corporation rules by creating an impermissible shareholder.

Permitted year. IRS Rev. Proc. 2002-38. Provided that the taxable year of an ESOP S corporation must be a "permitted" year, meaning a calendar year except in very limited circumstances. Fiscal year S corporations where the ESOP owns a majority, but not all, of the capital stock of the corporation may not use the exception that permits the corporation to retain the taxable year of its sole owner (i.e., the ESOP). It appears these corporations must now change their fiscal years to the calendar year unless they petition the IRS and receive approval to retain their fiscal years. Companies that retained their fiscal year and did not use the automatic approval process may be eligible for grandfathering under the ruling.

Temporary ownership of shares. PLR 200122034: Ruled that transient ownership of shares by an ESOP participant receiving a distribution from an S ESOP and rolling them into an IRA will not cause a violation of the prohibited ownership rules for S corporations.

Earnings on unallocated shares. PLR 200014043: Ruled earnings on unallocated shares can be used to repay an ESOP loan.

Right to elect benefit form. IRS Final Regulations (T.D. 8806): Final regulations ruling that the amendment of an S corporation ESOP to eliminate participants' right to elect benefit distributions in the form of company stock does not violate the protected benefit rules under Section 411(d)(6).

Reconversion. PLR 199952072: Ruled that a company that converts from S to C status in order for sellers to an ESOP to take advantage of Section 1042 tax deferral treatment cannot then reconvert to S status before five years have passed. The ruling also noted that the company could not become a qualifying S corporation subsidiary if acquired by an S corporation within five years.

Repayment of loan. PLR 199938052: Ruled that earnings on allocated shares in an S corporation cannot be used to repay an ESOP loan, but earnings on unallocated shares can (this was later changed by legislation; current law allows earnings on either kind of shares to be used to repay a loan).

Repayment of loan. PLR 199948038: In a second ruling on the issue of using earnings on ESOP shares to repay an S ESOP corporation loan, the IRS ruled that earnings on unallocated shares could be used. This ruling did not address the issue of earnings on allocated shares.

Tacking period. PLR 200003014: Ruled that company stock will constitute "qualified securities" under Section 1042 and that the selling shareholders' holding period for purposes of the three-year holding period requirement prior to sale to an ESOP will include the period during which the company was an S corporation.

Distributions in S corporations are not annual additions. In PLR201424030 (March 20, 2014), the IRS ruled that distributions in a 100% ESOP-owned S corporation are not annual additions. The company will allocate the distributions based on relative share balance. The company said that its earnings exceeded its cash needs.

S Corporation ESOP Shares Should Have Basis Adjusted for Net Unrealized Appreciation Calculations. In Rev. Rul. 2003-27, 2003-1 C.B. 597, the IRS ruled that for the purpose of calculating net unrealized appreciation, the basis of shares on an S corporation ESOP trust must be adjusted in the same way as any other S corporation shares are adjusted. Distributions, for instance, decrease the basis for tax purposes, while certain income items increase the basis. The IRS ruled that "an employee stock ownership plan (ESOP) is required to adjust its basis in S corporation stock under § 1367(a) for the ESOP's pro rata share of the corporation's items. Upon the distribution of S corporation stock by an ESOP to a participant, the stock's net unrealized appreciation under § 402(e)(4) is determined using the ESOP's adjusted basis in the stock."

Sale of Stock to an ESOP (Including 1042 Issues)

Transfer to spouse. PLR 2010244005**:** Ruled that an individual's transfer of ESOP qualified replacement property to his spouse in connection with their divorce will not trigger a taxable gain under Code § 1042(e)(1).

Tacking period. PLR 200827018: Allowed two selling shareholders of a C Corporation to include the time period that they owned a predecessor LLC that was merged into a newly created C Corporation in the three-year required holding period.

Transfer to trust. PLR 200709011: Allows a transfer of qualified replacement property to a Grantor Retained Annuity Trust to qualify for Section 1042 treatment provided that the taxpayer is treated as the owner of the qualified replacement property held in the in the trust and certain other conditions are met.

Definition of operating company. PLR 200337003: Ruled that an active real estate business can be organized and operated as an "operating corporation" under Section 1042(c)(4)(B) of the Code. The effect is to allow rollover investments from the sale to an ESOP to be used for real estate investment if properly structured.

Substantial compliance. Internal Revenue Bulletin 2003-37: States that have notary requirements for selecting qualified replacement property would be satisfied if the taxpayer's statements of purchase are notarized not later than the time the taxpayer files an income tax return following the purchases of qualified replacement property, as long as the purchases are made within the qualified replacement period.

LLC/partnerships. PLR 14642701 (2002): A limited liability company (LLC) owning stock in a C corporation can take advantage Section 1042 of the Code if it sells to an ESOP. (146427-01 is a temporary control number pending the assignment of a permanent PLR number by the IRS, but we were unable to locate that number).

Substantial compliance. PLR 200234003: A taxpayer who has substantively but not literally complied with the requirements of Section 1042 for documenting qualified replacement property is still be eligible for tax deferral treatment.

Restructuring. PLR 200125010: Ruled on a complicated integrated transaction in a closely held company with multiple owners and multiple classes of stock in which shares were exchanged among the owners and an ESOP ended up as the ultimate buyer. The IRS concluded that the redemption of the shares as part of the integrated transaction should be treated as a capital gain, not a dividend.

Transfer to partnership. IRS Revenue Ruling 2000-18: The IRS ruled that transferring qualified replacement property (QRP) to a partnership in exchange for an interest in that partnership is a disposition of the QRP and results in taxation.

Restructuring. PLR 200052023: Ruled that an acquisition of all of the outstanding stock of an unrelated target corporation in an exchange for stock of the acquiring corporation with an ESOP was a valid tax-free reorganization. The ruling also indicated that the transaction qualified the seller for Section 1042 deferral of gain treatment. While this PLR indicated this relatively straightforward approach to such a transaction would qualify, advisors currently favor reverse mergers or, more often, the creation of an ESOP in the target and the subsequent merger of the two ESOPs.

Substantial compliance. PLRs 199927003, 199934006, 199934007, 199934008, 199944009, 199944025, 9821022, 9852004, 9846015, 9735046, 9619065, 9550014, 9438016, 9429017, PLR 9028082, and 201144040: This series of PLRs all ruled that substantial taxpayer compliance with the requirements of Section 1042 were sufficient qualify for tax-deferral of capital gains even though the replacement property section had not been properly notarized.

Convertible preferred. PLR 9836022: Ruled that convertible preferred stock received in a recapitalization immediately before a sale to an ESOP would qualify as common stock and thus be an eligible employer security under ESOP requirements. Moreover, the stock would not be "Section 306" stock subject to ordinary income taxation immediately upon the exchange.

Stock options. PLR 9830028: Ruled that the sale of stock acquired pursuant to the exercise of nonstatutory stock options acquired before Section 83 of the Code was enacted in 1969 would be eligible for tax deferral treatment under Section 1042 of the Code. Note that this is an unusual case—options acquired after that date are not eligible for tax deferral.

Transfer to family limited partnership. PLR 9846005: Ruled that shares transferred to a family limited partnership and then sold to an ESOP were eligible for tax deferral treatment under Section 1042 of the Code, and that the three-year holding period requirement tacked on the years the shares were held by the owners who made the transfer.

Qualified replacement property. PLR 9720026: Ruled that the common stock of a new corporation formed by the seller to an ESOP in a separate company he owned will be considered qualified replacement property.

Transfer to charitable trust. PLRs 9715040, 9547023, 9533038, 9515002, 9438021, 9438012 and 943802: Ruled that the transfer of qualified replacement property to a charitable remainder trust does not cause the taxpayer to recapture the gain that was deferred following the sale of stock to an ESOP.

Restructuring. PLR 9721022: Ruled three companies owned by two shareholders could be combined into a holding company, and the owners could then each sell 15% of the holding company's stock to an ESOP and qualify for Section 1042 treatment and not be subject to excise taxation.

Failure to buy qualified replacement property. PLR 9644024: Ruled that a failure to buy qualified replacement property before death means there is no step-up in basis for the prior unrecognized gain and that the purchase of qualified replacement property by the estate after the death would not qualify for tax deferral.

Restructuring. PLR 9639071: Ruled that the merger of a 401(k) plan that allowed employees to buy stock in the company with an ESOP so that the combined plan would own over 30% of the company's shares would qualify the merged plan's ownership for the 30% requirement for a tax deferred sale to an ESOP.

Restructuring. IRS Technical Assistance Memoranda 9631002 and 9631003: The IRS ruled that the selling shareholders in a company were entitled to nonrecognition of gain treatment under Section 1042 of the Code upon the sale of stock to a company-sponsored ESOP, even though immediately thereafter the company's ESOP was merged into the ESOP of another company (Company B), and later Company A was acquired by Company B. The method here is a common one for ESOP transactions, with the acquiring company financing a new ESOP set up in the target company, then the two ESOPs merging. The purpose here is make sure the sale qualifies the sellers to the ESOP (owners of the target) for capital gains treatment and, as a result, the ability to defer taxation on those gains by reinvesting in qualified replacement property.

Transfer to charity. PLRs 9547022, 9547023 and 9515002: Ruled that the donation of qualified replacement property acquired after a sale to an ESOP and contributed to a charitable remainder unitrust does not constitute a disposition of assets requiring a recapture of taxes on the gain from the sale.

Transfer to charity. Private Letter Ruling 9533038: Ruled on a number of issues concerning the transfers of qualified replacement property acquired after a sale to an ESOP to a charity and a grantor trust. These do not constitute dispositions of the assets, which would otherwise require a recapture of taxes on the gain from the sale.

Partnerships. IRS Technical Advice Memorandum 9508001: Ruled that a partnership itself, not the individual partners, must make the election to treat a sale to an ESOP as qualifying under Section 1042 of the Code and that the partnership, not individual partners, must purchase the qualified replacement property within the applicable replacement period.

Transfer to charity. PLR 9542040: Ruled that the periodic sale of company common stock by a charitable remainder annuity trust to an ESOP to pay an annuity to the donor and family members specified by the trust do not trigger excise taxes even though the donor and the family members (but not the ESOP) are disqualified persons with respect to the trust because the amounts involved are very small.

Transfer to trust. PLR 9411003: Ruled that the distribution of qualified replacement property from a grantor trust to its beneficiaries would not constitute a disposition of assets causing a recapture of the gain from the sale to an ESOP. The trust had received shares in a closely held company then sold them to an ESOP and reinvested the proceeds in qualified replacement property.

Basis. PLR 9339005: Ruled that the basis of qualified replacement property is stepped up at death and that the transfer to the estate does not constitute a disposition of the assets subject to capital gains tax recapture.

Transfer to trust. PLR 9327080: Ruled that the transfer of qualified replacement property to revocable trust will not be treated as a disposition of assets subject to capital gains tax recapture.

Qualified replacement property. PLR 9432009: Ruled that if more than 50% of a company's assets were used in the active conduct of the company's trade or business then that company's stock would qualify as qualified replacement property under Section 1042 of the Code.

Restructuring. PLR 9312067: Ruled that the sale of stock in one corporation to the corporation's ESOP in exchange for a promissory note, and the contribution of the note plus any cash received during the "qualified replacement period" to another corporation in exchange for newly issued stock of the second corporation, qualifies for nonrecognition of gain treatment under Code Section 1042.

Taxable gift. PLR 9117035: Ruled that a son's decision not to exercise an option to buy his father's shares for $1,370 per share, and the father's subsequent sale of the shares to the ESOP for $5,502, constituted taxable gift to the father for the difference.

Basis. PLR 9109002: Ruled that the value of the shares sold to an ESOP are as of the time of the sale, not the time of the death of the person originally owning the stock.

Multiple seller sale. PLR 9041071: Three owners in a company sold an aggregate of 30% of the company's shares to an ESOP and chose nonrecognition treatment. One of them was a less than 25% owner. The company proposed to allocate shares from the other two sellers' shares to this employee (but not his own shares). The IRS ruled this was not acceptable because this was all of the same transaction in which the employee chose nonrecognition treatment.

Valuation. DOL No. 1990-04A: DOL Advisory Opinion allowed for sale of stock to an ESOP where there is an appraised fair market valuation.

Moving Qualified Replacement Property into Grantor Trust Is Not a Disposition Under Section 1042. In PLR 202206009 (Feb. 11, 2022), the IRS ruled that a taxpayer who sold stock to an ESOP and took the capital deferral treatment available under Section 1042 of the Code will not be treated as having made a disposition of the qualified replacement property purchased after the sale into a grantor trust the taxpayer controls. The IRS ruled that "Section 673 [of the Code] provides that the grantor shall be treated as the owner of any portion of a trust that the grantor has a reversionary interest in either the corpus or the income therefrom, if, as of the inception of that portion of the trust, the value of such interest exceeds five percent of the value of such portion."

Securities Law

Sales by participants. SEC Release, Charles Schwab Company (June 10, 1993); SEC Release, Commercial National Financial Corp. (available October 19, 1993); and SEC Release, Commercial National Financial Corp. (available October 19, 1993): All ruled that sales of stock by ESOP participants are not subject to Section 144 of the 1933 Securities Act, which requires people who receive shares in a private transaction in a public company to register the sales with the SEC and meet various other reporting, holding, and sales restrictions.

Voting. IRS Revenue Ruling 95-57: Ruled that a trustee is not prohibited from voting allocated shares for which no directions have been received in a timely manner from ESOP participants.

Appendix: Key Issues in DOL Settlement Agreements in GreatBanc, First Bankers Trust, James Joyner, Alpha Investment, Lubbock National Bank, and Farmers National Bank Cases

Perez v. GreatBanc Trust Co., C.D. Cal., No. 5:12-cv-01648-R-DTB, consent order and judgment, June 2, 2014 (GreatBanc Trust Company as trustee) (the "GreatBanc agreement")

Acosta v. First Bankers Trust Services, Inc., Maran, Inc., et al., S.D.N.Y., No. 1:12-cv-08648-GBD, consent order and judgment, Sept. 21, 2017 (First Bankers Trust Services as trustee) (the "FTBS agreement")

Related cases:

Acosta v. First Bankers Trust Services Inc., D.N.J., No. 12-4450, consent order and judgment filed Sept, 25, 2017 (First Bankers Trust Services as trustee)

Acosta v. First Bankers Trust Services Inc. S.D.N.Y., No. 12-8649, consent order and judgment filed Sept. 25, 2017 (First Bankers Trust Services as trustee), amended after appeal in *Acosta v. First Bankers Tr. Servs., Inc.*, No. 3:12-cv-04450-MAS-DES (D.N.J. consent order Nov. 19, 2017)

Acosta v. Bat Masonry Company, W.D. Va., No. 6:15-cv-00028-EKD-RSB, consent order filed Sept. 29, 2017 (James F. Joyner III as trustee) (the "Joyner agreement")

Acosta v. Mueller et al., E.D. Wi., Civil Action No. 2:13-cv-1302-PP, consent order entered Dec. 27, 2017 (Alpha Investment Consulting Group LLC as trustee) (the "Alpha Investment agreement")

Acosta v. Cactus Feeders, Inc., et al., N.D. Tex., Civil Action No. 2:16-cv-00049-J, settlement agreement entered May 4, 2018 (Lubbock National Bank as trustee) (the "Lubbock agreement")

Farmers National Bank of Danville and Weddle Bros. Construction Company, No. 1:20-cv-674 (SD Ind., Feb. 28, 2020) (the "FNB agreement").

In 2014, the U.S. Department of Labor (DOL) entered into a settlement agreement with GreatBanc Trust in settlement of a lawsuit concerning GreatBanc's actions as trustee to the Sierra Aluminum Co. ESOP, including a detailed fiduciary process agreement to be followed whenever GreatBanc serves as an ESOP trustee. The GreatBanc agreement created the template for future settlement agreements, each of which offered only minor variations on the GreatBanc agreement. The NCEO has a detailed book on the agreements.[1] This discussion just looks at their key features.

[1] Theodore M. Becker, Richard J. Pearl, and Allison Wilkerson, *The DOL Fiduciary Process Agreements for ESOP Transactions* (NCEO, 2021) (see www.nceo.org/r/agreements).

The agreements set forth a process to be followed when each of the affected trustees does ESOP work. They are not regulations, but do provide useful guidance on how the DOL thinks trustees should act.

The agreements have several key elements, as described below. All of the elements of the GreatBanc agreement are included in the subsequent ones. Note that the Lubbock agreement is identical to the original 2014 GreatBanc agreement and does not have any of the additional items introduced in the subsequent agreements.

Valuation Assessment

The GreatBanc agreement states that the trustee must "prudently investigate the valuation advisor's qualifications" and take "reasonable steps to determine that the valuation advisor receives complete, accurate, and current information necessary to value the employer securities." It also must determine "that its reliance on the valuation advisor's advice is reasonable before entering into any transaction in reliance on the advice." The appraiser should not have valued the stock that is to be the subject of the transaction with the ESOP for a party to the transaction other than the trustee. The FBTS agreement added that trustees need to document why they chose the appraiser and how they vetted the appraiser's qualifications. The Joyner agreement says this vetting must be repeated every 24 months, not the 15 in the GreatBanc agreement. This need not be done every time, however, for appraisers used regularly by the firm. The trustee should know the qualifications of the person actually doing the work, not just the firm.

One of the more important parts of the GreatBanc agreement concerns the specific documentation a trustee should ask for from the appraiser. These include looking at a number of specific metrics on projected financial performance and how they compare over the prior five-year prior period as well as to comparable public company data, if any. The measurements described are fairly standard in good ESOP appraisals; the agreement specifies what to look for and document.

The GreatBanc agreement also provides that the appraiser's report or trustee's documentation should demonstrate consideration of how "plan document provisions regarding stock distributions, the duration of the ESOP loan, and the age and tenure of the ESOP participants may affect the ESOP sponsor's prospective repurchase obligation, the prudence of the stock purchase, or the fair market value of the stock." This underscores an emerging but not yet universal practice to consider repurchase obligations and other distribution issues in connection with the appraisal.

The GreatBanc agreement requires that the trustee evaluate the debt for the transaction and the company's ability to repay it. It also requires that the trustee consider the fairness of the transaction with respect to such issues as whether the cost of the debt is reasonable. The FTBS agreement lays out additional guidelines for when an ESOP can pay a control price, requiring that the ESOP pay for actual control, not control that may be constrained by other agreements.

The GreatBanc agreement states a clear preference for audited company financial statements in connection with the appraisal. If the company's financial statements are not audited, the trustee needs to document why it is reasonable to rely on unaudited financial information.

In the FNB agreement, the DOL and FNB agreed on a sweeping definition of what elements of control the ESOP must have in order to pay for control. This goes well beyond what case law and standard practices have used, and it is unclear whether the DOL will use this as a standard elsewhere. The "right to control" is defined as including "all of the unencumbered rights that a shareholder would have that acquired the shares to be purchased by the ESOP, and the right to control the company's direction," including but not limited to:

- the unencumbered ability to vote its shares;
- the ability to appoint and remove the company's officers;
- the ability to appoint and remove the majority of the company's board of directors;
- the ability to set management compensation and perquisites;
- the ability to acquire, lease, or liquidate the company's assets;
- the ability to liquidate, dissolve, sell, or recapitalize the company;
- decision-making authority over mergers, acquisitions, and sales of company stock;
- authority to decide whether the company incurs significant debt or engages in debt refinancing;
- the ability to authorize or veto major capital expenditures;
- the ability to decide whether to sell or acquire Treasury shares and whether to declare and pay cash and/or stock dividends;
- the ability to determine whether to call warrants or other significant company obligations; and
- the ability to modify or amend the company's articles of incorporation or bylaws.

Loan Structure

The Alpha Investment agreement provides that where seller financing is used (as it was there), but outside financing was available, the fiduciary should evaluate whether the outside financing provided better terms, and, if so, why seller financing was used.

Providing the Right Information to the Appraiser

The GreatBanc agreement provides that the trustee should document that any information, including financial projections, that are provided to the appraiser is reasonable. The trustee should also document that it has considered a list of 16 different items in the valuation report, including assumptions as to various discounts, adjustments to financial projections made by the appraiser, the weighting of various methods of appraisal, discount rates, treatment of debt, assessment of the company relative to markets and the industry, and other standard elements of ESOP appraisals. The trustee also should document the specific steps taken to assess the valuation report as well as who did the work. That should include a discussion of the questions asked and areas of disagreement and how they were resolved.

The FBTS agreement added that trustees must ensure that the valuation advisor obtains information about any prior defaults within the past five years by the ESOP under any lending or financing agreement, plus any management letters provided to the ESOP sponsor by its accountants within the past five years. The trustee must document the identities of trustee employees who participate in decisions about the transaction, and those employees must document their work. If any of the trustee's employees who are primarily responsible for the transaction believe the valuation report's conclusions are not indicative of the company's true value, the trustee shall not proceed with the transaction.

The FNB agreement states that FNB must "[e]xplain any material differences between the present valuation and the most recent prior valuation of the plan sponsor performed within the past 24 months by any valuation firm for any purpose (if any exist). For valuations obtained exclusively by the sellers in connection with the transaction within the past 12 months, Farmers Bank "should at a minimum obtain information on when the valuation was performed and who prepared the valuation." The valuation advisor must obtain from the sellers: (1) all prior attempts by the purchasing or selling shareholder(s) to purchase or sell their stock in the plan sponsor within the preceding two years; (2) all prior defaults within the past five years by the plan sponsor under any lending or financing agreement; (3) all management letters provided to the plan sponsor by its accountants within the past five years; and (4) all information related to a valuation of the plan sponsor provided to the Internal Revenue Service within the past five years.

The GreatBanc agreement also provides that "the trustee will consider whether it is appropriate to request a claw-back arrangement or other purchase price adjustment(s) to protect the ESOP against the possibility of adverse consequences in the event of significant corporate events or changed circumstances." A "claw-back" generally requires that the seller returns some of the price it received for stock it sold in the event the value of the stock goes down significantly during a specific period of time after the transaction. It is difficult to get a seller to agree to such a provision, but the agreement states that the trustee should document in writing its consideration of the appropriateness of a "claw-back or other purchase price adjustment(s)."

Indemnification

The FNB agreement prohibited FNB from agreeing to indemnification provisions by the ESOP or the ESOP-owned company that result in the advancement of attorneys' fees and expenses unless "an entirely independent third-party determines that there has been no breach of fiduciary duty" and "a prudent arrangement" is in place that guarantees, through the posting of collateral or otherwise, a refund of the entirety of the advanced fees and costs should a fiduciary breach be determined by the court.

About the Author

Corey Rosen is the NCEO's founder and former executive director and now is its senior staff member. Corey has spoken on various subjects related to employee ownership all over the world with government, business, and union leaders, and he is regularly quoted in leading magazines and newspapers. He has appeared on national television and radio programs and also has authored four books on employee ownership, plus more than 100 articles for various business, academic, and professional publications. He has authored or coauthored several of the NCEO's practical and research publications. He holds a PhD in political science from Cornell University.

Made in United States
North Haven, CT
04 November 2026

21753011R00028